Preventing Prejudice

MULTICULTURAL ASPECTS OF COUNSELING SERIES

SERIES EDITOR
Paul Pedersen, Ph.D., *University of Alabama at Birmingham*

EDITORIAL BOARD

VOLUMES IN THIS SERIES

Preventing Prejudice

A Guide for Counselors and Educators

Joseph G. Ponterotto
Paul B. Pedersen

Multicultural Aspects of Counseling Series 2

SAGE Publications
International Educational and Professional Publisher
Newbury Park   London   New Delhi

For information address:

 SAGE Publications, Inc.
2455 Teller Road
Newbury Park, California 91320
E-mail: order@sagepub.com

SAGE Publications Ltd.
6 Bonhill Street
London EC2A 4PU
United Kingdom

SAGE Publications India Pvt. Ltd.
M-32 Market
Greater Kailash I
New Delhi 110 048 India

Printed in the United States of America

Library of Congress Cataloging-in-Publication Data

Ponterotto, Joseph G.
    Preventing prejudice: a guide for counselors and educators/
Joseph G. Ponterotto, Paul B. Pedersen
        p.   cm.   —(Multicultural aspects of counseling series; 2)
    Includes bibliographical references and index.
    ISBN 0-8039-5284-8   — ISBN 0-8039-5285-6 (pbk.)
    1. Prejudices—United States.   2. Prejudices in children—United
States.   3. Race awareness in children—United States.   4. Racism—
United States—Psychological aspects.   5. Race discrimination—
United States—Prevention.   6. Cross-cultural counseling—United
States. I. Pedersen, Paul, 1936- . II. Title. III. Series:
Multicultural aspects of counseling; v. 2.
BF575.P9P64   1993
305'.083—dc20   93-17333

02   03   04   05   06   07   10   9   8   7   6

Sage Production Editor: Diane S. Foster

Contents

Acknowledgments

We would like to acknowledge and thank those people who either directly or indirectly supported our writing and research efforts. First, our sincerest thanks to Marquita Flemming at Sage Publications for her unwavering support and enthusiasm for our efforts on this book and on the *Multicultural Aspects of Counseling Series* in general. We are indebted to our distinguished team of reviewers: Professors Norman D. Sundberg, Man Keung Ho, and J. Manuel Casas. These scholars devoted many hours to reviewing our material, and they provided helpful and constructive feedback. Thanks to them, our book is much improved over initial drafts. A special acknowledgment goes to Man Keung Ho who passed away in 1992. His contributions to this volume and to the series have been significant and are much appreciated. A distinguished scholar and a warm and caring person, he will be sorely missed.

A special thanks is also extended to Professor Clemmont E. Vontress who graciously prepared the *Foreword* to this volume. Dr. Vontress's contributions to the field of multicultural counseling and education are legendary, and we are honored by his contribution to and endorsement of this book.

Many individuals at our home universities need to be acknowledged for their support. At Fordham University, Drs. James Hennessy, Anthony Cancelli, Sheldon Marcus, Max Weiner, Judith Mills, and the Reverends Vincent Potter and Joseph O'Hare supported Dr. Ponterotto's Faculty

Fellowship during the Fall 1992 semester. A special thanks goes to Dr. Merle Keitel and the counseling faculty who ran the counseling programs during Dr. Ponterotto's leave.

Finally, we acknowledge the secretarial support and friendship of Mary Dailey and Joan Zangari at Syracuse University and Sr. Marian Mythen and Mimi Barkey at Fordham University.

The authors gratefully acknowledge permission to quote from the following:

Charles R. Ridley (1989), "Racism in Counseling as an Adverse Behavioral Process." In P. B. Pedersen, J. G. Draguns, W. J. Lonner, & J. E. Trimble (Eds.), *Counseling across cultures* (3rd ed.) (pp. 55-77). Honolulu, Hawaii: University of Hawaii Press. Permission granted from the publisher to adapt Table 1, p. 61.

Joseph G. Ponterotto (1991), "The Nature of Prejudice Revisited: Implications for Counseling Intervention." *Journal of Counseling and Development, 70,* 216-224. Permission granted from the publisher, the American Counseling Association, to reprint select paragraphs.

To Ingrid, my partner and best friend.

J. G. P.

To Anne Bennett Pedersen, my favorite teacher and life partner.

P. B. P.

Foreword

Carl Jung's collective unconscious is one of the most provocative ideas of Western psychology. The famous psychologist maintained that humans are not only products of their personal histories but also of the heritage of the human species. Genetic traces of previous generations motivate, shape, and influence the development of those who are yet to come. Cultural counterparts of similar ideas are also posited by anthropologists and sociologists. Books and articles that discuss the impact of cultural heritage on human behaviors are abundant. For example, we hear often the expression "Judeo-Christian heritage" to convey the notion that there is a way of life peculiar to Jews and Christians that dates back several centuries. It seems tenable to conclude that individuals unified by powerful similarities also transmit from one generation to another behavioral predispositions and responses peculiar to the collectivities in the same way that the human species does. That is, race-related cultures develop for various reasons. When they do, it is not unusual for such groups to consider their people and way of life to be superior to other peoples and their realities. In a sense, culture and its various aspects are defensive measures in place to ensure the safety, well-being, continuation, and often the domination of other racial and ethnic collectivities.

There are many other interesting observations that can be made about culture. It is important to recognize that it is conscious and unconscious and visible and invisible. It is something that we feel. We need not think about it. We are our culture. It is the language we speak, the clothes we wear, the values we hold, the ideas we have about the world, our fellows, and ourselves. Culture is these things and much more. Although we take it for granted, it dictates our total existence from birth to death.

Since culture is basic to humankind's survival, it is simultaneously defensive and offensive, depending on whose survival and well-being are at stake. In each culture, there are good and bad aspects that reside side by side and compete for supremacy. In our society, prejudice and racism are a part of the American cultural heritage, but they are defined by public policy as bad and inconsistent with the American Dream, not only for the victims but also for the victimizers.

Humans need to feel good about themselves. They retreat from accusations of wrongdoing, especially when that behavior is a product of their collective unconscious or cultural heritage and therefore invisible to them, because "that's the way it has always been." Although Americans who are victims of racial bigotry continue to document the many ways it stifles their existence, the accused victimizers seem unable to accept the indictment on a personal level or to modify their behavior. That is why *Preventing Prejudice: A Guide for Counselors and Educators* by my professional colleagues, Professors Joseph G. Ponterotto and Paul B. Pedersen is so important to counselors and educators, groups whose work influences significantly how people perceive reality. Other than parents, their contributions to the socialization of young people and, indeed, people of all ages are perhaps more important than any other definable group in our country.

This book is an important event for the counseling profession, which has been tardy in identifying and launching attempts to overcome impediments to effective counseling of ethnically and racially different people. In our profession, many concerned people continue to discuss such concepts as resistance, transference, and acting-out behaviors, as if to suggest that when counselors are unsuccessful with minority clients it is the client's fault. In the past, when it has been suggested to counselors that prejudice and racism might be a problem, some of them have retorted indignantly, "Yes, but you know, I am a counselor," as if to say that counselors are somehow immune to human imperfections that encumber the rest of us.

In schools, teachers berate their reluctant learners and frequently point to various aspects of their students' culture to explain their own inability to teach the way they have been trained. Few stop to explore the remnants of their own cultural heritage which may be impeding the learning process.

This book is also important because it is written by two Euro-Americans who care enough to want to prevent prejudice. Usually, African Americans and other minorities write books and articles calling attention to racism and its far-reaching implications for human existence. Seldom have whites addressed the topic such that large segments of the public have been willing to take direct action to change the society in the interest of all people, unless of course, the national interest was at stake. The Emancipation Proclamation issued by President Abraham Lincoln in September, 1862, effective January 1, 1863, by which all persons held in slavery in the Confederate States were freed, is a good example. The Civil Rights Act of 1964 may also be cited as an example of Americans acting in the interest of the whole—of everybody.

Indeed, the challenge that Ponterotto and Pedersen have taken on in writing this book is an awesome one. I applaud them for their courage and foresight. I congratulate them for providing counselors, teachers, and others with a valuable instrument for changing the way we look at ourselves and others. It is through changing understandings and perceptions that we change behavior. I am optimistic that a lot of good will come out of their contribution.

Clemmont E. Vontress
George Washington University

Preface

Current events document the pervasive and destructive nature of prejudice and racism in the United States and abroad. As we approach the twenty-first century where the global community becomes more interdependent and where the United States becomes increasingly heterogeneous, the need for concentrated attention to intergroup relations becomes obvious. As the reader will note in the introductory chapters, negative racial prejudice is a widespread universal phenomena, and it is not likely that prejudice could ever be completely prevented or eliminated. Yet, consistent and careful attention given to the topic by counselors and educators can result in improved race relations.

Preventing Prejudice: A Guide for Counselors and Educators presents a model and mechanism for improving interracial and interethnic relations. This book emphasizes the need for multicultural awareness programs to be preventive, developmental, and long-term. A comprehensive theoretical context of racial and ethnic identity development serves as the foundation for planning and directing multicultural programs.

To understand the complex nature of racial prejudice and racism, an interdisciplinary perspective is needed. In order to provide readers with a comprehensive understanding of prejudice and to equip them with directions for intervention, this book draws on theory and research in social psychology, developmental psychology, sociology, education, cross-cultural psychology, and counseling psychology.

Consistent with the **Multicultural Aspects of Counseling Series,** this volume is scholarly, up-to-date, and pragmatic. The book is organized into four major parts. Part I, "Understanding Prejudice and Racism," includes three chapters that provide the reader with the requisite background and overview for understanding prejudice and racism. Part II, "Racial/Ethnic Identity Development," consists of two chapters that provide the theoretical context for work in multicultural awareness and prejudice prevention. A pragmatic emphasis is the focus of Parts III and IV. Part III, "Race Awareness Strategies for the School and Community," includes four chapters that outline intervention roles for counselors and educators and a series of developmentally sequenced exercises and activities. Finally, Part IV, "Prejudice Prevention: Assessment, Research, and Resources," presents the final two chapters, which provide an overview of leading assessment instruments and resources for use in multicultural work. Two full instruments with scoring directions are presented in the Appendices.

We believe it is important for counselors and educators to be more fully trained in multiculturalism and more involved in prejudice prevention work. We hope *Preventing Prejudice* stimulates interest, research, and activity in this important field.

Joseph G. Ponterotto
Paul B. Pedersen

PART I

Understanding Prejudice and Racism

Part I of *Preventing Prejudice* introduces the reader to the topic of prejudice and racism. The three chapters comprising this section provide the necessary background for understanding the theoretical conceptualizations and pragmatic interventions specified in subsequent sections. Chapter 1 presents a rationale for the book and defines key terms used throughout the text. Chapter 2 focuses on the prevalence and consequences of racism and highlights the debilitating effects of prejudice and racism for all those directly or indirectly involved. Finally, Chapter 3 traces the development of prejudice from early childhood and outlines how prejudice is expressed both in attitudes and behavior.

Civilized men [women] have gained notable mastery over energy, matter, and inanimate nature generally, and are rapidly learning to control physical suffering and premature death. But, by contrast, we appear to be living in the Stone Age so far as our handling of human relationships is concerned.

(Allport, 1954, p. xiii)

1

Prejudice and Racism: Introduction and Definitions

The quote on the preceding page was taken from Gordon W. Allport's (1954) book, *The Nature of Prejudice*. In the 40-odd years since the book was published, hundreds of articles, books, and films have addressed the issue of prejudice. Furthermore, numerous empirical studies have been undertaken in the hope of clarifying how prejudice develops and how it can be combated. Despite this scholarly attention to the topic, prejudicial attitudes and racist behaviors are as common today as when Allport addressed the topic some forty years ago. In fact, many social scientists would argue that prejudice and racism are on the rise in recent years. Consider the following recent events in the United States and abroad.

- In April of 1992, four White Los Angeles police officers were acquitted of a [discretely videotaped] assault of an African-American motorist, Rodney G. King. The acquittal ignited riots and violence in south-central Los Angeles. The approximate toll of the riots was 50 deaths, 1,600 businesses completely destroyed or severely damaged, and financial losses approaching $800 million (Mydans, 1992; Mydans & Marriott, 1992).
- The National Institute Against Prejudice and Violence documented (through nationwide newspaper clippings) 105 incidents of college campus

3

ethnoviolence in 1988, and 109 incidents during 1989 (Ehrlich, 1990; Pinkow, Ehrlich, & Purvis, 1990).

* *USA Today* reported the following "hate crime" statistics for the United States in the year 1991: 25 murders, 101 cross burnings, and 216 acts of vandalism ("When tensions rise," 1992).

* During September and October of 1992 there was a wave of neo-Nazi attacks on refugee dwellings in at least 10 East German Cities (Kinzer, 1992). As of this writing, at least 10 people had been killed, and the planned attacks were escalating.

* In October of 1992 the United Nations established a War Crimes Commission to investigate claims of "ethnic cleansing" (ethnic and cultural genocide) in war ravaged Bosnia-Herzegovina.

These current events serve as a frightening reminder that prejudice and racism continue to pervade the world society. Although the violence in Bosnia and East Germany may seem distant to the American reader, the collapse of international borders coupled with continued advances in global communication bring these significant international events closer to home. More than anything else, *Preventing Prejudice* serves as a call to all counselors and educators to become more informed and involved in prejudice prevention work.

Purpose and Focus of This Book

The overall purpose of this book is to provide mental health professionals and educators with an in-depth understanding of prejudice and to equip them with specific guidelines for intervening in the area of prejudice prevention and remediation. Specifically, we attempt to present prejudice within an understandable historical and theoretical context so that prevention program goals and methods can be carefully thoughtout and appropriately implemented and evaluated.

Prejudice can be directed at any number of groups and can be race-based (racism), gender-based (sexism), age-based (ageism), or ethnic-based (ethnocentrism), among others. Although much of the contents of this book is relevant to all forms of prejudice, our particular focus is on racial and ethnic prejudice. By focusing on limited forms of prejudice we will be able to provide in-depth coverage of the issues while also specifying pragmatic interventions.

Prejudicial attitudes and beliefs also transcend national boundaries and can be found among every "people" of the world. Our focus in this text is on prejudice as a widespread phenomenon in the United States. Notwithstanding this focus, research and literature from other countries will be incorporated into our discussions when a more international perspective helps to clarify a relevant concept or position.

This book is written primarily for professional counselors and educators working at all developmental levels (with children, adolescents, and adults) and in a variety of settings (e.g., primary and secondary schools, colleges and universities, and the community at large). *Preventing Prejudice* will also be of value to mental health professionals in general (e.g., psychologists, social workers, psychiatrists), to administrators and personnel managers in all settings, and to graduate students in these specialty areas.

Definitions: Part 1

It is important to clarify and define key terms used throughout this book. This first section on definitions examines the following terms: *race, ethnicity, culture, minority, majority,* and *racial/ethnic minority groups.*

Race

Popular definitions of race have conceptualized the term within a biological classification system. Krogman's (1945) often-cited definition is a good example: "A sub-group of people possessing a definite combination of physical characters, of genetic origin, the combination of which to varying degrees distinguishes the sub-group from other sub-groups of mankind [womankind]" (p. 49).

Simpson and Yinger (1985) summarize commonly recognized physical characteristics that distinguish one race from another: skin pigmentation, nasal index and lip form, and the color distribution and texture of body hair. Commonly recognized racial types are Caucasoid, Mongoloid, and Negroid (Atkinson, Morten, & Sue, 1989).

In a recent review of race terminology, Ponterotto and Casas (1991) highlight concerns with regard to the focus on race as a biological classification. Race-based distinctions tend to categorize people, yet there are more differences within racial groups than between them. Atkinson et al. (1989) highlight that the term *race* has no biological consequences, but what people believe about race has profound social consequences. The concern here is that through subtle socializing influences, people come to accept as "social fact" the myriad stereotypes about a group of people based solely on their skin color, facial features, and so forth. Farb (1978) notes that race-based physical characteristics (e.g., skin color, hair texture) have no genetic relation to intelligence or personality, notwithstanding that such beliefs have been an assumption by people in Western societies.

Pedersen (1992), in reviewing the international literature (e.g., Miles, 1989; Segal, Dasan, Berry, & Poortinga, 1990), concludes that the race construct has been discredited as a scientific and biological term, but that it remains an important political and psychological concept. Other writers (e.g., d'Ardenne & Mahtani, 1990; Phillips & Rathwell, 1986) have highlighted that the race concept has been used as a political pawn by the power-dominant group in maintaining the oppression of minority groups. A good example of this is in the area of racial differences in intelligence tests. Pedersen (1992) reviews the work of Segal et al. (1990) and comes to the conclusion that research on so-called racial differences in intelligence has a long and distressing history. He notes that much of the thinking about race and intelligence has been irrational, politically motivated, and very costly in human terms. Pedersen highlights the psychological damage resulting from erroneous beliefs regarding the causes of so-called race-based differences in intelligence.

It is clear, therefore, that the reader must keep in mind the social and political complexity of race terminology as the contents of this book are read and absorbed. For our present purposes, racial groups include White Americans, African Americans, Asian Americans/Pacific Islanders, and Native Americans. Hispanics can belong to any of the aforementioned groups. Although our classification system is rather simplistic and does nothing to solve the terminology dilemmas just reviewed, it does allow us to integrate past research on *race* into our current discussion.

Ethnicity

Ethnicity has been conceptualized by Rose (1964) as a group classification of individuals who share a unique social and cultural heritage (e.g., language, custom, religion) passed on between generations. Here the focus does not rest on a biological or genetic foundation as was the case for *race* (Ponterotto & Casas, 1991).

Our preferred definition is given by Yinger (1976) who defines *ethnic group* as follows:

> A segment of a larger society whose members are thought, by themselves and/or others, to have a common origin and to share important segments of a common culture and who, in addition, participate in shared activities in which the common origin and culture are significant ingredients. (p. 200)

Using this definition, Ponterotto and Casas (1991, p. 10) provide a specific example clarifying the distinction between *ethnic group* and *race:* "Jews, given their shared social, cultural and religious heritage are an ethnic group; they are not, however, a race" (see also Thompson & Hughes, 1958).

Culture

The term *culture* has often been used in the literature as synonymous with *race* and *ethnic group*. However, there are distinctions between the terms. For example, the White American group is made up of many diverse ethnic groups, such as Irish, Polish, Jewish, Italian, and so on. Within these ethnic groups may lie a diversity of cultures predicated by such factors as length of time living in the United States, socioeconomic status, religion, sexual orientation, geographic locale, and so on. Given this diversity between *and* within human groups we prefer the broad definition of *culture* put forth by Linton (1945): "The configuration of learned behavior whose components and elements are shared and transmitted by the members of a particular society" (p. 32).

Minority

One of the most popular terms heard in everyday language today is *minority* or *minority group*. This term has direct relevance to our discussions throughout this book, and our usage of the term parallels the definition of *minority* put forth by Wirth (1945):

> A group of people who, because of physical or cultural characteristics, are singled out from others in society in which they live for differential and unequal treatment, and who therefore regard themselves as objects of collective discrimination. . . . Minority status carries with it the exclusion from full participation in the life of the society. (p. 347)

The central focus of this definition is on the lack of social, political, and economic power/influence faced by certain groups in American society. The definition does not necessarily revolve around numerical representation in society. For example, females in the United States constitute 53% of the total population. They represent the numerical majority, but, by our definition, they are also a *minority group* in the sense of the economic and political power they hold (see also Ponterotto, Lewis, & Bulington, 1990).

Majority

To speak of a *minority group* implies by its very nature the existence of a contrasting group—the *majority group*. The majority group (sometimes referred to as the dominant or mainstream group) is that group which holds the balance of power, influence, and wealth in society. The majority group in the United States consists of the White population generally, and, more specifically, White middle-class males (Ponterotto et al., 1990).

Our present usage of the term *majority group* incorporates not only White, Anglo-Saxon Protestants, but also White ethnic groups. A rationale for this grouping is provided by Ponterotto and Casas (1991), who note that although most White immigrant groups were confronted with prejudice and oppression when first arriving in America, their experience in the United States has been qualitatively different than the experiences of non-White people. These authors point out that because of their more Anglo features (mainly White skin), White ethnics were allowed eventually (sometimes by changing their last name) to assimilate and become part of "mainstream" America. This was not the case, however, for people of color, who, because of their physical differences, have been blocked from fully participating in the "land of opportunity."

Our position that all White Americans, regardless of ethnic or cultural background, belong to the majority (or dominant) group is further supported by Pettigrew (1988; cited in Essed, 1991, p. 29) who speaks to the unique experiences of Black Americans:

> In a significant way, European immigrants over the past century and Blacks face opposite cultural problems. The new Europeans were seen as not "American" enough; the dominant pressure on them was to give up their strange and threatening ways and to assimilate. Blacks were Americans of lower caste; the pressure on them was to "stay in their place" and not attempt assimilation into mainstream culture of the privileged. (Pettigrew, 1988, p. 24)

Racial/Ethnic Minority Groups

This book focuses on the differential power-influenced relationship between the majority group in the United States (i.e., White Americans) and racial/ethnic minority groups (i.e., African Americans, Hispanic Americans, Asian Americans/Pacific Islanders, and Native Americans). For the purposes of accuracy and clarity, the term *racial/ethnic minority* group is the term that best captures these specified groups (Casas, 1984). *Racial* incorporates the biological/heredity classification; *ethnic* incorporates classifications of individuals who share a unique social and cultural heritage; and *minority* reflects the lower economic, political, and social status conferred upon specific groups by the White majority (Ponterotto & Casas, 1991).

Definitions: Part 2

This section defines three terms central to this text: Prevention, prejudice, and racism. Given that the book has a *prevention* focus, it is important to specify our usage of the term. Furthermore, the terms *prejudice* and *racism* have often been used interchangeably in the literature. Although there is overlap in the meaning of the terms, there are fine distinctions. This section also takes an in-depth look at these two terms and clarifies our preferred definitions for their use.

Prevention

An important focus throughout this text is prevention—preventing the potential escalation and expressions of racial prejudice. Prejudice is a common phenomenon of human nature, and it is unrealistic to think we can completely prevent it. However, it is feasible to stem the tide of increasing prejudice, and, in fact, to facilitate a decrease in prejudicial attitudes regarding race and ethnicity.

Empirical and conceptual literature on prevention in mental health is plentiful and found primarily in the discipline of Community Psychology (e.g., Albee, Bond, & Monsey, 1992; Felner, Jason, Moritsugu & Faber, 1983; Hermalin & Morrell, 1987; Hess & DeLeon, 1989; Kessler, Goldston, & Joffe, 1992; Lorion, 1990; Roberts & Peterson, 1984). A popular construct within this body of literature is the tripartite model of prevention: Primary, secondary, and tertiary levels.

Primary prevention "refers to intentional programs that target groups of currently unaffected people for purposes of helping them to continue functioning in healthy ways, free from disturbance" (Coyne, 1987, p. 6). Therefore teaching young children to appreciate and welcome cultural diversity would serve as an example of primary prevention. Secondary prevention refers to early detection of problems followed by immediate interventions. Thus, for example, an elementary school teacher might hear prejudicial remarks made by her or his fifth graders and decide that a unit on tolerance and multiculturalism is in order. Finally, tertiary prevention refers to interventions after serious problems have emerged. An example might be counselors called into a community or school where race-based physical violence has erupted. In summary, the goal of primary prevention is to prevent problems from developing, whereas the goal of secondary and tertiary prevention is to prevent the escalation or continuation of problems that have developed.

Although counselors and educators are involved in all three forms of prevention, the model stressed in this book is *primary prevention*. We propose in later chapters that by incorporating multicultural relations training throughout the developmental life-span, people will have a greater understanding and appreciation of their own culture and the cultures of others. A result of effective developmental interventions is improved inter-racial and inter-ethnic relations in the United States. Our focus on primary prevention is consistent with the traditionally espoused roles of professional counselors and educators (discussed in Chapter 6).

Prejudice

Allport (1979) provides a thorough and clear conceptualization of the term *prejudice*. Historically, the word *prejudice* stems from the Latin noun *praejudicium,* meaning a precedent or judgment based on previous decisions and experiences. According to Allport (1979, p. 6), prejudice can be defined using a unipolar [negative] component, as in "thinking ill of others without sufficient warrant"; or incorporating a bipolar [negative and positive] component as in "a feeling, favorable or unfavorable, toward a person or thing, prior to, or not based on actual experience." Both of these definitions include an "attitude" component and a "belief" component. The attitude is either negative or positive, and the attitude is tied to an overgeneralized or erroneous "belief."

Although prejudice can hold either a positive or negative tone, racial and ethnic prejudice in the United States has taken on primarily negative connotations (Allport, 1979; reviewed in Ponterotto, 1991). Our emphasis in this book is on prejudice as a negative phenomenon. Our usage of the term *prejudice* parallels Allport's (1979) often-cited definition for *nega-*

tive ethnic prejudice: "Ethnic prejudice is an antipathy based upon a faulty and inflexible generalization. It may be directed toward a group as a whole, or toward an individual because he [or she] is a member of that group" (p. 9). This definition contains three key components worth specifying. First, prejudice is negative in nature and can be individually or group focused. Second, prejudice is based on faulty or unsubstantiated data. Third, prejudice is rooted in an inflexible generalization (Ponterotto, 1991). This last point is particularly important because the inflexible nature of a prejudice makes it highly resistant to evidence that would contradict it. For our purposes, prejudice includes internal beliefs and attitudes that are not necessarily expressed or acted upon. Racism, on the other hand, has an "action" or behavioral component.

Racism

According to Dovidio and Gaertner (1986b) the term *racism* became popular in the American lexicon after its use in the *Report of the National Advisory Commission on Civil Disorders* (1968). This well-known report cited racism by Whites as a factor in the disadvantaged plight of many Blacks in America. Since the publication of this report numerous scholars have elaborated on the term *racism*. One scholar who has devoted extensive research efforts to the study of racism is James M. Jones (1972, 1981, 1986, 1988) of the University of Delaware. Jones defines racism as follows: "[Racism] results from the transformation of race prejudice and/or ethnocentrism through the exercise of power against a racial group defined as inferior, by individuals and institutions with the intentional or unintentional support of the entire culture" (Jones, 1981, p. 28).

Jones (1972, 1981) specifies three forms or levels of racism. *Individual racism* is conceptualized as a person's race prejudice based on biological considerations and involving actual behavior that is discriminatory in nature. *Institutional racism* includes the intentional or unintentional manipulation or toleration of institutional policies (e.g., school admission criteria, taxes) that unfairly restrict the opportunities of targeted groups. *Cultural racism* is the more subtle form of racism and the most pervasive and insidious. This form of racism includes the individual and institutional expression of the superiority of one race's cultural heritage (and concomitant value system) over that of other races. Therefore, the majority value system summarized by Katz (1985) and elaborated upon in recent texts

(Pedersen, 1988; Ponterotto & Casas, 1991; Ponterotto et. al., 1990) serves as a foundation for cultural racism when it is perceived as the "model" system, and when those individuals who possess alternative value systems are thought of by the White majority as being deficient in some way.

A more recent [and counseling-focused] look at the definition and scope of racism as been provided by Ridley (1989), who builds upon the work of Jones (1972). It is Ridley's conception of racism that most closely parallels the thinking of the present authors, and, therefore, his landmark work will be covered in some detail. Ridley (1989) defines *racism* as "any behavior or pattern of behavior that systematically tends to deny access to opportunities or privilege to one social group while perpetuating privilege to members of another group" (p. 60).

Ridley emphasizes the terms *behavior* and *systematic* in his definition. *Behavior* implies human action that is observable and measurable. *Systematic* implies that the consequences of racist behavior are predictable and occur repeatedly. Included in Ridley's (1989, pp. 57-58) conception of racism are five assumptions:

1. Racism is reflected in behavior.
2. Racist acts can be performed by nonprejudiced as well as prejudiced people.
3. Racism is not the sole responsibility of a single racial or ethnic group.
4. The criteria for judging whether or not a behavior is racist lies in the consequences, not the causes, of the behavior.
5. Power is a force that is absolutely essential to perpetuate racism.

Ridley (1989) distinguishes between individual and institutional racism. His distinctions are similar to those outlined by Jones (1972) and reviewed earlier in this Chapter. Individual racism involves the harmful behavior of one person or a small group of individuals. Institutional racism involves the harmful effects endemic to institutional structures or social systems. These categories can be further broken down into smaller units of analysis based on whether the behavior is overt or covert, and whether it is intentional or unintentional. Tables 1.1 and 1.2 (adapted and expanded from Ridley, 1989, p. 61) present a matrix depicting these distinctions in the contexts of counseling and education.

In examining these tables, the reader will note that overt acts of racism are always intentional—the intentionality is defined by the behavior. Covert racism, by contrast, can be intentional or unintentional. Tables 1.1 and 1.2 provide specific examples of each form of racism.

Table 1.1 Varieties of Racism in Counseling

	Individual Racism	Institutional Racism
Overt (Intentional)	Counselor believes that racial/ethnic minorities are inferior and, on this basis, refuses to accept them as clients.	Counseling agency openly denies services to racial/ethnic minority clientele.
Covert (Intentional)	Counselor assigns a racial/ethnic minority client to a student intern because of social discomfort but claims to have schedule overload.	Counseling agency deliberately sets fees above the affordable range of most lower- and middle-income minority families, thus effectively excluding them from counseling.
(Unintentional)	Counselor misinterprets a minority client's lateness and lack of eye contact as resistance to the counseling process.	Counseling agency uses standardized psychological tests without considering the relevance and validity of the tests to culturally diverse clients.

SOURCE: Reprinted from Ridley (1989, p. 61) and adapted with permission of the publisher.

The Racism-Prejudice Distinction

Our usage of the term *racism* throughout this book parallels that of Ridley (1989). We are concerned with the effects and consequences of harmful behaviors directed towards certain racial/ethnic groups. Our conception of *prejudice* focuses on an attitude or belief that is negative and based on a faulty and inflexible generalization. Race-based prejudice often leads to racist behaviors—but not always. A person can have race-based prejudices but not act on them. Similarly, not all racist behavior stems from individuals who possess race prejudice. Using Ridley's (1989) definition, people who are well-intentioned and relatively free of race prejudice can unintentionally engage in behavior that is racist (i.e., has negative consequences for the group) (again refer to Tables 1.1 and 1.2 for specific examples).

It is our view that no single racial/ethnic group has a monopoly on prejudice and racism. Prejudice transcends all racial/ethnic groups in the United States and all nations of the world. For this reason, combating prejudice is *everyone's* responsibility.

In spite of this view, however, much of our focus in this book examines the individual and institutional racism of Whites and White-controlled institutions. We maintain this focus for three reasons. First, as noted earlier, *power* is the force that drives racism, and the White [particularly

Table 1.2   Varieties of Racism in Education

	Individual Racism	*Institutional Racism*
Overt (Intentional)	An elementary school teacher believes minority students are less motivated and, therefore, intentionally assigns these students to the less desirable and challenging classroom activities.	The administration of an elite private college believes minority students would ultimately detract from the school's "prestige" and therefore prohibits college recruiters from visiting high schools with large minority student enrollments.
Covert (Intentional)	A high school assistant principal assigns a majority of African-American students to the most disliked teachers because she/he believes these students cannot really be taught, anyway.	An elite high school deliberately sets tuition fees above the affordable range of most lower- and middle-income minority families, thus effectively excluding them from the school.
(Unintentional)	An elementary school teacher misinterprets a minority student's non-assertiveness and lack of eye contact as an indication of the student's non-interest in school.	A doctoral program in psychology uses a high score on the Graduate Record Exam as an admission cutoff score without considering cultural influences in standardized testing.

SOURCE: Adapted with permission from Ridley (1989, p. 61).

male] majority clearly holds the balance of power in the United States. Second, in the relatively brief history of race relations in the United States, White Americans and White-run institutions and policies have been the prime perpetrators of racism. Third, the majority of psychological research on the topic has focused on White racism.

Our position is that although all people need to be involved in the fight against prejudice (see also Miles, 1989; Pedersen, 1992), White Americans, particularly, must acknowledge their past and present racism and take a proactive lead in combating all forms of racism (see, particularly, Bowser & Hunt, 1981; Helms, 1992; Katz, 1978).

An important point to emphasize here is that one does not have to be "actively racist" to contribute to the racism problem. Many segments of American society (e.g., Whites, men, the affluent, nondisabled) enjoy benefits, privileges, and opportunities not available to groups with traditionally less power in society (e.g., persons of color, women, the poor, the disabled). These past and continuing inequities in treatment affect crucial quality-of-life categories, such as educational access, income, health services, housing, leisure opportunities, etc. (see Jones, 1986). In the long-run, these inequities have negative consequences for *all* Americans. Therefore, it behooves all segments of society to eliminate them.

Chapter Summary

Chapter 1 highlighted the fact that prejudicial attitudes and racist behaviors are common in the United States and around the world. There is some evidence that racial prejudice and acts of racism may be escalating. It is clear that racism continues to be a major concern of the modern world, and it is apparent that more effective and carefully thought-out modes of combating prejudice and racism are needed.

This chapter also clarified a number of definitions that are central to the discussion throughout this book. The current usage of two important concepts, *prejudice* and *racism*, have been highlighted.

Chapter 2 examines the prevalence and consequences of racism. It sets out a strong rationale for increased counselor and educator involvement in the areas of prejudice prevention and race relations.

2

Prevalence and Consequences of Racism

With the constructs of prejudice and racism defined in Chapter 1, this chapter examines the prevalence and seriousness of racism, the evolving nature of racism, and the "gains" that maintain racist behavior. If counselors and educators are to work effectively in the area of prejudice/racism reduction, an accurate understanding of the problem is necessary. This chapter concludes by introducing the counselor's role in prejudice prevention work.

The Prevalence of Racism

Interreligious, interethnic, and interracial animosity can be traced back to early human history. Conflict over religion, physical appearance, beliefs, and customs of people from different ethnic groups has been and will continue to be a primary source of unrest in the world (Landis & Boucher, 1987; Stagner, 1987). In an edited book on *Ethnic Conflict*, Boucher, Landis, and Clark (1987) document interethnic and interracial conflict throughout the world.

To assess the present status of race relations in the United States one simply needs to turn on the nightly news or read the daily newspaper. Incidents of race-based tensions and conflicts can be found throughout the country. "Bias incidents," "bias attacks," or "hate crimes" (as they are popularly called in the media) appear to be on the rise in recent years. Increasing racial tensions can be found in high schools (Sherman, 1990), on college campuses (Ponterotto et al., 1990), and in the larger community (Sue & Sue, 1990). It is clear that racism is a widespread problem in the United States. Exact figures on what percentage of the U.S. population is prejudiced or racist are not available. Some earlier research estimated the percentage of Whites who were prejudiced towards Blacks. In his often cited review of extensive survey data from multiple sources, Pettigrew (1981) found that roughly 15% of White adults are extremely racist, largely due to authoritarian personality needs. Approximately 60% of White adult Americans are conforming bigots, reflecting the racist ideology of the larger society. Finally, about 25% of White adults consistently support rights for Blacks and can be said to be antiracist in ideology and behavior.

These data are somewhat disconcerting. Only 25% of the White population appear to take a stand against racism. Although only 15% of the samples were extremely racist, 60% of White Americans conform to racist ideology in society. By not being part of the solution, this 60% is part of the problem. Therefore, 75% of the population, to some degree, promotes the status quo, which is racial inequality. Pettigrew (1981) emphasizes that White Americans increasingly reject racial injustice in principle but remain reluctant to accept and act on measures necessary to eliminate the injustice.

The Pettigrew (1981) research sheds some light on the magnitude of the prejudice problem in the United States. His research, however, is more than 10 years old; moreover, it focuses only on prejudice exhibited by one racial/ethnic group (White Americans). Research is needed on the prevalence and manifestations of racism among other racial/ethnic groups. Furthermore, more extensive research is warranted on the prevalence of racism generally, regardless of racial/ethnic group.

The Evolving Nature of Racism

The face of racism has changed. Overt racism is on the decline, but "newer" forms of racism continue to thrive—and may be on the increase. A distinction can be made between "older" and "newer" forms of racism. The racism most familiar to Americans and most likely to be covered in the media is the older form, known as "old-fashioned racism" (Greeley & Sheatsley, 1971; McConahay, 1982), or "dominative racism" (Gaertner & Dovidio, 1986; Kovel, 1970). This form of racism is evident in individuals who act out bigoted beliefs, those who represent the open flame of racial hatred (Gaertner & Dovidio, 1986).

The outright expression of racism in the United States has declined in recent years (Katz & Taylor, 1988), due in part to the social stigma attached to racism and to increased consciousness-raising among some segments of the population. According to McConahay (1986) two historical changes have contributed to the decline of old-fashioned racism and to the emergence of modern racism. First, the bad name Hitler gave racism inhibited its open expression. Second, the success of the Civil Rights movement legitimized the concept of equality of opportunity.

The new form of racism has been called "modern racism" (McConahay, 1986; McConahay & Hough, 1976), "aversive racism" (Gaertner & Dovidio, 1986), "symbolic racism" (Sears, 1988), and "new racism" (Jacobson, 1985). The root of *modern racism* is in a continuing Eurocentric philosophy that values mainstream (dominant-culture) beliefs and attitudes more highly than culturally diverse belief systems. (For the most recent and comprehensive historical analysis of prejudice the reader is referred to Duckitt, 1992a, 1992b.)

The modern racist believes that discrimination no longer exists and that minority groups are violating cherished values and making unwarranted demands for changing the status quo (Sabnani & Ponterotto, 1992). Modern forms of racism can also be seen in those majority group Americans who possess strong egalitarian values, sympathize with the victims of past injustice, support policies that promote racial equality, regard themselves as nonprejudiced and nondiscriminatory, but who possess negative feelings and beliefs about minority groups.

One major theme pervading the newer conceptions of prejudice is that racist attitudes and beliefs are outside conscious awareness. Given that racist views contradict most people's stated value system, one's view of self would be impacted negatively if a racist ideology were acknowledged. Therefore, holding racist beliefs out of conscious awareness keeps the self-concept intact.

Acknowledging that modern racism is subtle and often beyond conscious awareness, it can be assumed (consistent with Pettigrew's [1981] findings discussed earlier) that a large percentage of White Americans are modern day racists. The average citizen who swears he or she is not racist depicts racism as an intentional, overt act—that is, the old fashioned type. And, given most Americans don't engage in overt racist acts, they believe they are not racist. We know, however, from Chapter 1 that racism can also be covert and unintentional; it can be very subtle. Although we continue to hear of bias incidents and overt racism, the majority of racism today is of the covert and subtle form. The view of many social scientists is that you cannot be socialized into a society stratified along racial lines and not be influenced by a racist ideology (Ponterotto, 1991; Skillings & Dobbins, 1991; Sue, 1992; Sue & Sue, 1990).

Consequences of Racism

The overt effects of racism on the target group are easy to identify. Eight million Jews were slaughtered as a result of Nazi anti-Semitism and worldwide disinterest and inaction. Roughly eight million Africans died or became permanently disabled during their forced voyage to America (Skillings & Dobbins, 1991). Hundreds of Americans lost their lives in the twentieth century as a result of lynchings, bombings, beatings and other acts spawned by racial hatred.

Less obvious, but equally insidious, are the new forms of racism. Modern, yet deadly, they can drain the lifeblood from its target. In the 1990s one can still find subtle (and at times overt) race-based discrimination in housing, education, and employment. Focusing on Black-White relations, Jones (1986) maintains that White racism is a major contributing factor in the disparity between Whites and Blacks in crucial quality-of-life categories—health, education, and crime. Confronted with continuing oppression from the power-dominant group, target group members can develop coping and defense mechanisms that although helpful in some ways, can be harmful in other ways (see extensive discussion in Allport, 1979; Simpson & Yinger, 1985).

Consequences of Racism on the Racist

When people think of the consequences of racism, they usually focus on the traumatic effects for the victim or target of racist behavior. However, as Pedersen (1992, p. 6) notes: "racism brutalizes and dehumanizes both its object and those who articulate it." Racism effects us all, whether we are the victims, the perpetrators, or simply the witnesses.

In his presentation of revealing autobiographical sketches of Whites growing up in the South, Dennis (1981) demonstrates that the immersion of individuals in a racist social network makes it difficult for any White person to avoid its influence. Dennis (1981) extracts a number of effects of racial socialization on White children: (a) ignorance of other people, (b) development of a double psychological consciousness and moral confusion, and (c) group conformity.

Ignorance of Other People

Dennis (1981) points out that although many Whites think they "know" Blacks, what they really know is an "idea" of the Black. Dennis (1981, p. 74) quotes Boyle's (1962, p. 30) autobiographical sketch with regard to what she and her friends "knew" of Blacks: " Their virtues as well as their faults were fixed and exaggerated in my mind. Blacks were artistic and creative, content in hardship and ill fortune, loyal, faithful, and warm."

Building from the early work of Halsey (1946) and Clark (1955), Dennis (1981) notes that racism deprives Whites of getting to know Blacks and increases their ignorance of the diversity within the African American population.

Double Psychological Consciousness
and Moral Confusion

A duality of consciousness develops when one's humanistic values are challenged by racial socialization. For example, the subjects in Dennis's (1981) autobiographical sketches were taught to love everyone, but not Blacks, to respect the elderly, but not older Blacks. Parents' desires to create racial stratification are confusing to children. Dennis (1981, p. 76) quotes Boyle (1962, p. 22):

> I remember running into the house heartsick after snubbing the advances of a [Black] child of whom I was particularly fond. He had skipped up to me, suggesting that I come along on some small adventure. . . . Crushing back my desire both for his company and for fun, I answered stiffly, "No, I can't." Then I added with proper Southern-lady courtesy, "How are you?" My mother had watched the exchange. . . . she said, "Mother saw and heard everything. That was a good girl." A strong combination of depression and pride swept me. I was a GOOD GIRL. But, oh, what I had *done*!

Children are faced with moral dilemmas as they attempt to digest divergent norms and values. Dennis (1981, p. 78) outlines five contradicting values:

1. the desire to be a Christian versus the desire to be a traditional White Southerner,
2. the belief in freedom and democracy versus the belief in racial inequality,
3. the desire to show love and compassion versus the desire to keep Blacks in their place at all costs,

4. the belief in the Southern tradition of respect for the old versus the belief that older Blacks are not worthy of the highest respect,

5. the belief that each person should be treated according to his or her individual merits versus the belief that Blacks should be evaluated as a group without regard to individual merits and talents.

Group Conformity

Children learn at an early age how to conform to prevailing social norms of the family and the "in group." Dennis (1981) states that it is very unlikely that White children escape the pressures to conform to the prevailing racial etiquette. Dennis (1981, p. 77) reviews the work of Rosen and Rosen (1962) who relate the story of a 7-year-old boy who, after hearing his friends discuss the fact that a Black family had moved to the neighborhood ran home yelling to his mother, "Niggers are moving here! And we're going to get rid of 'em!"

Through parental and community pressure to conform to racial roles, White children become restricted in their world view. They come to depersonalize whole racial groups through the use of abstractions, as in "the Blacks," or "they," as if the group had no relation to their own existence. In addition to examining the impact of racism on White children, Dennis (1981) reveals some impacts of racism on the White population in general: Racism engenders irrationality, it inhibits intellectual growth, and it negates democracy.

Terry (1981) maintains that racism undermines and distorts White peoples' authenticity—being true to self and to the world. This leads White Americans to contradict their stated values in their daily behaviors, to distort power in relationships, to build organizations they neither understand nor run efficiently, and to misjudge and poorly handle human resources. Karp's (1981) psychological explanation of White racism takes on a psychodynamic flavor as she sees racism as a defense mechanism used to deal with past hurt. Her position, like that of Dennis and Terry, is that Whites are deeply hurt by their racism. It isolates Whites from persons of color and fosters a general isolation among Whites. False race barriers are erected which deny Whites friendships with non-Whites. Racism restricts Whites as they limit daily aspects of their lives, such as where to live, work, and play. Karp further maintains that racism keeps different groups of Whites (e.g., women, the working class) from recognizing who their true allies are.

Racism leaves Whites with a distorted picture of reality. As Karp (1981) notes, the emotional consequences of racism are heavy:

> A major result of racism for Whites is guilt and shame, along with feeling bad about being White (sometimes expressed as a flip side—rigid pride in superiority). Lacking any other explanation for their racist feelings, people either defend their attitudes as "natural" (piling many layers of confusion on top of their guilt feelings) or blame themselves. The ability to think constructively about racism and to find solutions to it is thus hindered. Guilt especially tends to distort actions, often resulting in well-intentioned but nonetheless offensive (and harder to address) behavior. (p. 89)

Gains From Racism

Given the obvious destructiveness of racism to all people, what maintains it in today's society—a society that is highly educated and that prides itself on fairness and justice? This is a complex question with no easy answer. On one hand, there may appear to be tangible gains from racism for the racist. On the other hand, racism may be maintained because the ethnocentric ideology that fosters it pervades society. Racism, therefore, represents the status quo, and people fear change. This latter explanation for the maintenance of prejudice will be addressed in Chapter 3 where the origins and development of racism are reviewed. Below, we address some tangible gains associated with the racist's behavior.

Simpson and Yinger (1985) state:

> It seems unlikely that human beings would show an enormous capacity for prejudice and discrimination were it not for the gains they seem to acquire. To be sure, these may be primarily short-run individual gains, tied inextricably to serious long-run losses. (p. 156)

Ridley (1989) notes that racism confers tangible benefits upon the dominant group, for example, social privilege, economic status, political power, and even gains in "psychological feelings" (e.g., feeling special) (see also Axelson, 1985).

Simpson and Yinger (1985) outline four specific gains accruing to Whites as a result of prejudice and racism towards Blacks. These authors build on the earlier work of Dollard (1937), who studied White-Black relations in the Southern United States. Simpson and Yinger (1985) extend Dollard's work to more contemporary majority-minority power differentials. Gains for Whites were in the areas of economic, sexual, prestige, and status quo advantages.

Economic gains. From a purely financial standpoint, Whites profited greatly from slavery. Even today, the discriminatory treatment of migrant workers brings significant financial reward to landowners and company-owners. Billions of dollars each year accrue from a combination of wage, occupational, human capital, and labor monopoly discrimination. Furthermore, by keeping minority groups relatively powerless, dominant groups are able to reduce the necessity for their own employment in poorly paid, monotonous jobs (see also Allport, 1979).

Sexual advantages. According to Simpson and Yinger (1985) sexual advantages accrue to men in their power relations over women of minority groups. More globally, sexual harassment of women in general, both in education and in the work place, seems to be an endemic problem of the 1990s (Ponterotto et al., 1990).

Prestige. Most individuals want to be more than just "average" members of society. Many people need to feel special and important. Therefore, if an entire racial group can be kept in an inferior position and can be led to give signs of humility and deference, the oppressor gains a comfortable feeling of prestige.

Maintaining the status quo. Many people find change frightening and fear the unfamiliar. Even if there is a sense that a current behavior is wrong or harmful (e.g., racism), modifying or eliminating the behavior is difficult. The status quo, even if unhealthy, is familiar. Old, ingrained habits and views are hard to break, even in the face of contradictory evidence. Given that American institutions and culture are racist, rapid change is understandably challenging.

In presenting these four short-term gains typically associated with prejudice and racism, Simpson and Yinger (1985) emphasize the fleeting nature of the gains and the more significant damaging impact of racist behavior on all parties involved. It is beyond dispute that the negative consequences of racism for all involved far outweigh any fleeting gains for the oppressor.

Racism as a Disease

Racism is often thought of as a social problem. Like other social ills—homelessness and poverty, for example—racism is taken for granted, and people just accept that it will always be part of society. It appears that only a small percentage of the population expends energy trying to eradicate racism.

Although popularly acknowledged as a social problem, racism can also be thought of as a disease. Society seems to have an easier time dealing with a disease model. There are few moral overtones when dealing with disease; it is diagnosed and then treated. Billions of dollars are spent each year studying diseases and attempting to discover cures. Some writers believe that if racism were described as a disease, mental health professionals would be more likely to understand and devote energy to the topic (see Skillings & Dobbins, 1991). There is support for a disease model of racism.

Karp (1981) believes that racism is the result of early "hurt" experiences endured by the racist. She adheres to the Freudian notion that painful early childhood experiences become repressed and then eventually projected or displaced onto others. Therefore individuals are driven by unresolved early-life conflicts, and racism is a mental health problem [or mental disease] that needs to be addressed. In her own work, Karp (1981) uses counseling/support groups to provide a nonjudgmental environment where group members are led to process, work through, and eliminate racist feelings, attitudes, and behaviors.

A more recent conception of racism as a disease was posited by Skillings and Dobbins (1991). These authors point out that one cannot grow up in mainstream society without adopting the world views and biases of the society (see also Sue, 1992). Therefore mainstream people are socialized into an ethnocentric or racist mentality. Racists may not be responsible for "catching" the racist disease, but they are accountable for their behavior once infected, and they are responsible for their own treatment.

Skillings and Dobbins (1991) compare racism to a chemical addiction paradigm. A first step of treatment is to admit one has the disease. Denial, according to Skillings and Dobbins (1991), is a major symptom of racism as it is with substance abuse. Individuals need to work through their denial before they can begin to process the guilt and other emotional responses associated with racism therapy (see Skillings & Dobbins, 1991).

Chemical dependency is also conceptualized as a family disease. Although only one member of a family may be the identified alcoholic who drinks to excess, substance abuse counselors often tell members of the family that they *all* suffer from alcoholism. This statement is often met with denial and disbelief by the family members. Clearly, the whole family suffers in an alcoholic household. One cannot grow up in an alcoholic family without being profoundly influenced by what goes on around the alcoholic's behavior and the family's reaction to that behavior. Racism, too, is not just an individual disease; it is a group disease. In this case, the group is not the family but society. Although only a small percentage of Americans may be openly racist, those growing up in a racist society are bound to be affected by the disease. Skillings and Dobbins (1991), among many others (e.g., Dennis, 1981; Karp, 1981), believe that you cannot grow up in mainstream American society and not be infected by the "disease" of racism.

The Role of Counseling
in Prejudice and Racism Prevention

It is fair to say that the counseling profession has not been as involved as it could be in the prevention of prejudice and racism (D'Andrea, 1992; Ponterotto, 1991). Typically, when counselors are called upon to intervene in the area of race relations, it is after the fact; that is, after some bias incident has occurred in the school, on the campus, or in the community. Very often, these interventions are nothing but a Band-Aid, stemming the tide of racial animosities only in the short run.

Counselors and educators can have a powerful impact on human relations training generally, and racism awareness training specifically, if they devoted more time and study to the prejudice issue. Prejudice prevention must start with parent training, move into the elementary school and extend into the high school and beyond if the profession is serious about significantly reducing racial prejudice in society.

Some writers (e.g., Ponterotto, 1991) believe that the counseling profession has an ethical responsibility to increase its work activity in the prejudice and racism area. Although often seen as focusing on one-on-one relationships, counseling professionals have a multitude of skills and can work within a variety of modalities (e.g., small and large groups, families). Counselors can be very effective community change agents (see Atkinson, Thompson, & Grant, 1993), and with increased multicultural training they have the potential to impact the status of race relations significantly. Educators as well can and should play a major role in race-relations training.

Chapter Summary

This chapter has reinforced the need for increased study of prejudice and for more professional involvement in prejudice prevention. The evolving and changing nature of prejudice has been highlighted. Yet, whether conceptualized as old-fashioned racism or modern racism, the endemic problem remains. The consequences of this racism were explored in-depth and the effects of racism on both the target group and the perpetrator were discussed. Finally, the gains that cause people to maintain racist behavior were reviewed, and a call was made for increased counselor and educator involvement in race appreciation training. Chapter 3 now turns to a discussion of the development and expressions of prejudice.

3

Development and Expressions of Prejudice

Chapter 1 defined prejudice and racism, and Chapter 2 explored the magnitude and evolving complexity of the racism problem. Chapter 3 now turns to a closer look at the development and expressions of racial prejudice. If counselors are to design effective prejudice prevention programs, an adequate understanding of the developmental process associated with prejudice is necessary.

The Nature of Prejudice

Allport (1979) argues convincingly that humans have a propensity toward prejudice. Prejudicial views result easily from an interaction of three factors: our tendency towards ethnocentrism, our lack of significant intergroup contact, and our inclination to organize information into predeveloped categories.

Ethnocentrism

It is natural for people to cling to their own values and personal views and to hold them in high esteem. It is also common for people to prefer their own "in group"—family, religious group, ethnic group—to "out groups."

There are positive aspects to prejudice. People develop a sense of security and affiliation by identifying with a particular "in group." This can be seen in the teenager who joins a particular gang, or in the college athlete who associates almost exclusively with other athletes. Having a positive prejudice toward your own in group gives one the sense of belonging, identity, pride, and comfort.

Prejudice toward one's group can also serve as a survival mechanism. Groups that have been oppressed by the dominant society have had to rely on one another to cope with harsh and oppressive conditions. Native Americans, for example, could not trust the European settlers. Many promises (treaties) were made by the settlers to the Native peoples of America, and most of them were broken (Ponterotto & Casas, 1991). A positive prejudice toward their own tribal group and a concomitant distrust of the European settlers constituted, therefore, a healthy and justified coping response. Similar scenarios with other American minority groups, such as African Americans in slavery and Japanese Americans in internment camps, could also be used as relevant examples.

Often, however, and without sufficient warrant, people exaggerate the virtues of their own in group. Allport (1979) uses the term "love prejudice" to refer to peoples' tendency to overgeneralize the virtues of their own values, family, and group. Love prejudice toward one's own group can lead to antagonism toward outside groups, and thus serve as the foundation for ethnocentrism. Aboud (1987, p. 49) defines ethnocentrism as "an exaggerated preference for one's group and concomitant dislike of other groups." Ethnocentrism serves as a building block for negative racial prejudice (Ponterotto, 1991).

Lack of Significant Intergroup Contact

Separation between human groups is common throughout the world. People often prefer their "own kind" as a matter of convenience. Allport (1979, p. 17) asks, "with plenty of people at hand to choose from, why create for ourselves the trouble of adjusting to new languages, new foods, new cultures, or to people of a different educational level?" This preference to associate primarily with "like-minded" individuals leads to a form of cultural ignorance among many people. Without significant intercultural contact, people's perceptions of individuals representing other racial/ethnic groups is more often than not based on faulty information.

Relying on Ethnic Categorizations

As in-group preference and separatism among human groups is common, so, too, is the tendency to categorize and overgeneralize. To manage and cope with daily events in a highly technological, stimuli-loaded environment, individuals must process and sort extensive amounts of information. To do so quickly and efficiently, people rely on predeveloped categorizations. Unfortunately, due to a lack of intergroup contact and knowledge, cognitive categorizations formed with regard to racial and ethnic groups are often based on stereotypical information.

Early Formation of Racial Attitudes and Preferences

Above, we summarized the nature of prejudice in somewhat general terms. We have seen that prejudice can develop easily through the interaction of three factors common to many people throughout the world. This section takes a developmental and chronological look at the development of attitudes regarding race and ethnicity.

Children first come to recognize their racial/ethnic background at about 3 or 4 years of age (Aboud, 1987; Katz, 1987). From this time, until about the age of 7 or 8, children demonstrate increasing competence in perceiving their similarity to their own group. Children at this point can accurately categorize different groups based on perceptual cues (e.g., race, language), they can label groups consistent with adult labels, and they understand the consistency notion that race and ethnicity are unchangeable (see review by Ponterotto, 1991).

The expressed racial/ethnic attitudes and preferences of children across age levels have been researched. White children ages 4 to 7 consistently express a same-group ethnic preference and hold negative or moderately negative attitudes toward other racial groups. This is the case regardless of the research methodology employed to access the children's preferences (see Aboud, 1987).

Ethnic-attitude research on older children, ages 7 to 12, is less conclusive. Some research shows that negative attitudes continue up until about 12 years of age, whereas other research has found that prejudice declines after 7 years of age. In her extensive review of the empirical research,

Aboud (1987) explains that this decline in expressed prejudice may be due to perceived social desirability pressure experienced by the children. By this age, children are fairly perceptive in picking up cues from the researcher, family, or society generally, that prejudice (and expressed same-group preference) is not a desirable trait.

In reviewing research on the ethnic attitudes and preferences of Black children ages 3 to 8, Aboud (1987) found that 27% of the samples expressed same-group preference and negative attitudes towards Whites. These negative attitudes often remained high until about 12 years of age. Sixteen percent of the respondents expressed a White-identity preference; however, these preferences were neutralized or became anti-White with age. Finally, 57% of the Black children displayed no ethnic preference.

Although childhood research on racial/ethnic preferences provides some information on when and how children begin to express racial attitudes, it is important not to overinterpret the meaningfulness of such research. First, the results of later childhood studies can vary depending on the methodology used, the amount of exposure children have to other racial/ethnic groups, and the prevalent socioeconomic conditions in the household and community (see reviews in Phinney & Rotheram, 1987b). Second, racial attitude statements made by children may have different meanings than the same statements made by adults. Children's expressed attitudes are likely to be in part an artifact of the method used and the developmental stage of the child (Ponterotto, 1991). Katz (1987) stated that "the expression of prejudice in young children may reflect the child's perceptual and cognitive limitations more than any stable, organized predisposition to act in a certain way" (p. 93).

In his most recent work, Cross (1991) highlights the conceptual and methodological flaws of early research on Black self-identity. For example, previous research that found some Black children preferring to play with White dolls tended to be interpreted from a "Black self-hate" framework. A more appropriate explanation for such findings is that Black children may be socialized to be bicultural or culturally flexible (see Ramirez, 1991), whereas White children (who consistently expressed a preference to play with White dolls) are socialized to be monocultural or culturally inflexible. Therefore, one must be careful not to overinterpret or misinterpret research on racial preferences in children (see Cross, 1991; Phinney & Rotheram, 1987a).

Learning About Race

Earlier in this chapter we discussed Allport's (1979) view that prejudice can develop rather easily. Negative racial prejudice does not, however, develop in a vacuum. For children and adolescents to develop racial prejudice there must be either an implicit or explicit societal message of superiority or inferiority based on race. People have a need to be accepted by significant others, whether it is a child attempting to please his or her parents, a teenager wishing to be accepted by a peer group, or an adult looking for approval from a boss on the job. Given the pervasive nature of negative racial prejudice and modern racism, one must conclude that society is condoning racial inequality either directly through continuing discrimination or indirectly through its refusal to alter the status quo.

As we introduced in Chapter 2, although there are some tangible short-term benefits or gains for the dominant group in maintaining a racist ideology, our view is that racism is maintained primarily because there is little social and peer pressure within the dominant group to change the status quo. Furthermore, the average member of the dominant society thinks along the following lines: "Racism is just another social problem plaguing society, a problem that little can be done about, and certainly a problem that I cannot do anything about." Let us now examine some ways that children learn about acceptable social mores.

Parental Influence

Without question, the greatest influence on young children's attitude development are their parents. Young children rely on parents for security, comfort, and approval. Children learn quickly what behaviors, attitudes and values are likely to be met with either approval or disapproval from parents. If dominant-group parents believe that the White race is superior or "better" than other races, then children are very likely, and in short time, to acquire a similar racial attitude.

Parental behaviors that facilitate the development of negative racial prejudice in children include the following:

- Not discussing racial issues in the home (e.g., it's too touchy or sensitive to talk about)
- Not having a culturally diverse group of friends visit the house with regularity

- Not confronting prejudicial remarks when heard in the company of children—for example, remarks heard on television, or remarks made by neighbors or other children
- Allowing children to remain in segregated environments (e.g., attending an all-White school), or not making attempts to compensate for such isolation (e.g., interracial play groups)
- Not pointing out the positive aspects and strengths of diverse cultures, including their own

The Media

The media, in all its forms—print, news, entertainment—has a powerful influence on racial attitude development in the young and elderly alike. Children, adolescents, and adults develop perceptions of racial/ethnic groups consistent with the way members of these groups are portrayed (or not portrayed) in the media. For years racial/ethnic minority group members were seen only in limited roles, and often these roles were stereotypical in nature. Only in recent years have racial/ethnic minority group members begun to take more varied and less stereotypical roles.

Cultural depictions in the media that promote negative racial prejudice include the following:

- Portraying minority group members in stereotypical roles
- Not portraying minority group members in positive, leading roles, or simply not having minority members in visible positions (e.g., news anchor people)
- Highlighting criminal activities and tensions found in some minority communities while neglecting to cover the positive efforts and activities of minority communities

School System

The most pervasive influence on young children outside the family is the school environment. The American "school culture" has been criticized as fostering the status quo and catering to a White middle- and upper-middle-class constituency. Aspects of the school culture that promote the development of negative racial prejudice include the following:

- An administration and faculty that are not culturally diverse
- A student body that is not culturally diverse

- A learning environment that caters to only one value system—for example, individual achievement orientation as opposed to a group orientation, a competitive nature versus one of cooperation, a future time emphasis versus one that focuses on the past and present—all White middle-class value biases
- A curriculum that emphasizes European history and the dominant culture
- A school culture that does not incorporate training in race relations and sexism awareness as part of the curriculum.

World of Work

Racial attitude formation develops in the family, is nourished in the school environment, and continues on throughout the world of work. A company's or corporation's philosophy about diversity is passed down to all employees. If corporation executives tolerate racial and gender inequality, and if they are more likely to promote White men to leadership positions, then employees learn that differential treatment based on race and gender is normal and acceptable. More specifically, organizational behaviors that promote negative racial prejudice include the following:

- Not having minority group members in leading executive and management positions
- Fostering and rewarding only a middle-class, Western European-based value system
- Tolerating subtle racism and sexism at the workplace

Politics and Law

Federal legislation and Presidential Executive Orders can serve as powerful forces in both promoting a respect for cultural differences and decreasing prejudicial attitudes and racist behaviors. Allport (1979) provided convincing evidence that pro-equality Presidential Executive Orders and Supreme Court decisions, if enforced, serve as sharp tools in the battle against discrimination. It seems that although legislation is intended to control outward expressions of tolerance, such laws may, over time, affect inner attitudes and feelings.

On the other hand, if the government and courts fail to set racial equality precedents or waver in their support of affirmative action programs, then the population gets the subtle message that there is nothing wrong with the American system and the status of equal rights. Actions or inactions taken by the government that promote prejudice include the following:

- Not passing (or watering down) equal rights acts for minorities and women
- Halting affirmative action programs prematurely
- Downplaying or minimizing racial and sexual harassment charges

We have highlighted how major institutions "teach" negative racial prejudice. Learning prejudice is easy, and so is expressing prejudicial attitudes. However, expressions of prejudice can take many forms, as we discuss in the next section.

Expressions of Prejudice

Many people are prejudiced, but as the Pettigrew (1981) research discussed in Chapter 2 demonstrated, only a small percentage of individuals act on their prejudice. Prejudice can take various forms and expressions, ranging from the mild and covert to the harsh and overt. Allport (1979) presented a five-phase model of "acting out prejudice." His model presents expressions of prejudice on a continuum from least to most energetic. The five phases or levels are named *Antilocution, Avoidance, Discrimination, Physical Attack, and Extermination.*

Antilocution is the mildest form of prejudice and is characterized by prejudicial talk among like-minded individuals and an occasional stranger. This is a rather controlled expression of antagonism that is limited to small circles. As an example, a group of White neighbors may express fear that the neighborhood is becoming too integrated and that not only will their property values go down, but their children will more likely be exposed to aggressive peers.

Avoidance occurs when the individual moves beyond just "talking about" certain groups to conscious efforts to avoid individuals from these groups. The individual expressing avoidance behavior will tolerate inconvenience for the sake of avoidance. Thus, for example, instead of getting off at bus stop "z" and walking one block to work, this individual will get off at bus stop "y" and walk six blocks to work just to avoid the populace around bus stop "z." It is important to note that the inconvenience is self-directed, and the individual takes no harmful action against the group being avoided.

During the *Discrimination* phase, the individual takes active steps to exclude or deny members of another group entrance or participation in a desired activity. Discriminating practices in the past (and currently) have led to segregation in education, employment, politics, social privileges, and recreational opportunities (Ponterotto et al., 1990). Thus a White member of a cooperative housing board may vote against a Mexican American family attempting to secure housing. As another example, a faculty search committee member at a large institution may note that the department need not be focused on affirmative action efforts since "we hired a Black professor last year" (see related discussions by Wright, 1990).

The fourth phase of prejudice expression is *Physical Attack*. Under tense and emotionally laden conditions it does not take much for an individual to move quickly from the discrimination stage to physical confrontation. On any given day in any city newspaper, you are likely to read of race-based destruction of property or of an actual confrontation. From the high school grounds to the college campus to the city streets, we seem increasingly to hear of race-influenced confrontations and attacks (Ponterotto et. al., 1990; Sherman, 1990). There is some evidence that during stressful economic periods (e.g., the American recession of the early 1990s, or the rapid influx of refugees to East Germany in the early 1990s) physical attack becomes a more frequent expression of prejudice.

Extermination marks the final phase of Allport's (1979) five-point continuum. As the term implies, extermination involves the systematic and planned destruction of a group of people based on their group membership. Allport cites lynchings, pogroms, massacres, and Hitlerian genocide as the ultimate expression of prejudice.

Naturally, individuals at one particular phase may never progress to the next. However, increased activity at any one level increases the likelihood that an individual will cross the boundary to the next. Allport (1979) provides a poignant example:

> It was Hitler's antilocution that led Germans to avoid their Jewish neighbors and erstwhile friends. This preparation made it easier to enact the Nürnberg laws of discrimination which, in turn, made the subsequent burning of synagogues and street attacks upon Jews seem natural. The final step in the macabre progression was the ovens at Auschwitz (p. 15).

Chapter Summary

This chapter has taken a close look at the nature and development of racial prejudice. The goal of this chapter was to increase the reader's knowledge of the development and expressions of prejudice as well as the mechanisms by which people, particularly children, *learn* prejudice. Specifically, we examined how parents, schools, the media, work environments, and governmental policies contribute to the development of prejudice. Chapter 3 concludes Part I of *Preventing Prejudice*. The reader should now possess a deeper understanding of the nature and complexity of prejudice and racism. Building on this background, Part II presents a theoretical context for understanding racial/ethnic identity development, a critical factor in successful prejudice-prevention programming.

PART II

Racial/Ethnic Identity Development

The majority of race awareness exercises and prejudice prevention programs are not solidly grounded in accepted theory of interracial interaction. For this reason, many of them have met with only limited success. However, in the past decade, research on racial and ethnic identity development has enabled us to bring a new understanding to the nature of prejudice. Racial identity theory serves as a solid foundation for studying the origins, nature, and prevention of prejudice.

This section of *Preventing Prejudice* reviews the latest theory and research on racial/ethnic identity development. Chapter 4 reviews racial/ethnic identity models for African Americans, Hispanic Americans, and Asian Americans. Chapter 5 concentrates on models of White racial identity development. The relationship of racial identity development to measures of mental health and racism are explored. This section suggests that facilitating the development of a healthy and positive racial/ethnic identity among all Americans is a prerequisite to a tolerant, racially harmonious society.

4

Minority Identity Development and Prejudice Prevention

Mental health professionals and educators have been involved in prejudice-prevention programming for decades. Although we can assume some of these programs have been effective in attenuating negative racial prejudice, it is also fair to say that many of the programs have not been too effective. One concern with prejudice-prevention programs, in general, is that many of the interventions are remediative in nature and brief in duration (Ponterotto, 1991). It is common for race-awareness programs in schools, agencies, and business to range in length from a few hours to a few days. Our position is that it takes more than a few hours or days of sensitivity training to reverse years of ethnocentric thinking. A main point of this book is that race appreciation is a lifelong developmental process that begins with a healthy sense of one's own racial/ethnic identity. We must feel good about who we are before we can respect and feel good about others (see also Smith, 1989, 1991).

This chapter reviews and integrates both general and race/ethnic specific models of minority identity development. Research on the mental health correlates of various stages is summarized, and the relationship of prejudice to racial/ethnic identity is discussed. We begin our discussion of identity development by briefly reviewing the work of Erik Erikson and

James Marcia. With these conceptual models in hand, we move to a discussion of both general and race-specific models of minority identity development. The focus of Chapter 5 will be on White racial identity development.

Erikson's Model of Identity Development

Erik Erikson (1950, 1968) has provided a theory of ego identity formation. According to Erikson, an achieved identity results from a period of exploration and experimentation that usually takes place in adolescence. Working through the exploration, the adolescent comes to solidify decisions and commitments in various areas, such as religious ideology, occupational identity, and political orientation. James Marcia (1966, 1980) extended Erikson's work in his model of ego identity development. Marcia (1980) outlined four distinct ego identity statuses around the elements of crisis and commitment. His view is that to form an adult identity, each individual must experience a crisis in ideas derived from childhood identity development. The adolescent must explore possibilities, experiment with different options, and eventually make decisions and commitments about what to believe and what to become.

Marcia's Model of Identity Development

According to Marcia (1980) an adolescent is in the stage of *Identity Diffusion* if she or he has not experienced an identity crisis, engaged in exploration, nor made identity commitments in various areas. Marcia's second identity status is termed *Foreclosed Identity* and describes the adolescent who makes an identity commitment based on external influence carried on from childhood, without undergoing his or her own identity crisis and exploration. This unexplored commitment often is based on the values of parents, which were so influential in childhood.

The *Moratorium* status describes the adolescent in the midst of an identity crisis who is still exploring and experimenting with options but has not yet made a commitment to aspects of identity. This status is characterized by an active identity search. Finally, an *Achieved Identity* characterizes the individual who has had an identity crisis, has explored and experimented with options, and has now come to a commitment regarding what to believe and what to become.

A number of studies have correlated higher ego identity functioning (i.e., Achieved Identity, and Moratorium) with higher levels of psychological functioning (Phinney, 1990; Phinney, Lochner, & Murphy, 1990; Waterman,

1984). In a concise review of identity development in the college years, Delworth (1989) highlights that this positive mental health correlation is specific to males. Citing research of Schenkel and Marcia (1972), Delworth notes that when traditional commitments (i.e., occupation, political, and religious ideology) were extended to include sexual values and standards, the Marcia model was more applicable to women. Interestingly, this research found that the commitment aspect of the model was the distinguishing factor in correlating identity development to college women's mental health functioning. That is, women who had a committed identity, either an *achieved* identity or a *foreclosed* identity, had higher levels of self-esteem and lower levels of anxiety.

To explain these gender differences in identity development, Delworth (1989) integrates the work of leading theorists in the area of women's identity (e.g., Belenky, Clinchy, Goldberger & Tarule, 1986; Gilligan, 1982; Josselson, 1987; Miller, 1976). Delworth (1989) concludes that women's focus on the centrality of relationships and their caring ethic predispose them to a need to feel anchored. Citing Josselson's (1987) work specifically, Delworth (1989, pp. 164-165) states "Women who have anchored in their primary families choose to become 'purveyors of the heritage,' the essence of foreclosed status. Identity achievers tend to anchor in husband and children, friends, and career. Moratorium and diffused women are, then, anchorless, and thus outside the relational web so necessary for mature female development."

Much of the research examining how adolescents and young adults develop commitments to identity statuses has focused on identity in the areas of occupation, religion, political ideology, and gender roles. Much less research attention has focused on looking at racial/ethnic identity commitment levels. In the remainder of this chapter we focus on the importance of racial/ethnic identity development to the establishment of a healthy self-concept and positive intercultural attitudes. It is our contention that racial/ethnic identity development is as central to self as are the traditionally researched areas of identity development—namely career, political philosophy, religion, and gender role.

General Models of Minority Identity Development

This section reviews two general models of minority identity development. The Phinney et al. (1990) model extends the identity development work of Erikson (1950, 1968) and Marcia (1980) to race, ethnicity, and minority status. Using research in developmental and adolescent psychology as a base, Phinney et al. (1990) developed a stage model applicable to minority adolescents. The second model described in this section is the Minority Identity Development (MID) model of Atkinson, Morten, and Sue (1989, 1993). Atkinson et al. write from the perspective of counseling psychology and focus more on adults.

Phinney Model of Adolescent Ethnic Identity Development

The extensive work of Jean S. Phinney (1989, 1990; Phinney & Alipuria, 1990; Phinney et al. 1990; Phinney & Rotheram, 1987a; Phinney & Tarver, 1988) and her colleagues has provided a secure bridge linking ethnic identity development to more general models of adolescent identity development. Phinney et al. (1990) note:

> It is our thesis that a commitment to an ethnic identity is an important component of the self-concept of minority youth and a factor that mediates the relationship between minority status and adjustment. That is, adolescents who do not explore and take a stand on issues regarding their status as minority group members, nor develop a secure ethnic identity with which to obtain meaning and self-direction in an ethnically heterogeneous society, may be at risk for poor self-concept or identity disorders. (p. 54)

Phinney et al. (1990) suggest that minority group members need to resolve two primary issues or conflicts that result from their status as members of a nondominant group in society. The first issue is the existence of dominant-group stereotyping and prejudice toward their group. Phinney et al. (1990) review the work of Tajfel (1978) and Gibbs (1988), who note that individuals belonging to a group that is disparaged and stereotyped by the majority group face a threat to their self-concept. The second issue revolves around contrasting value systems. Minority individuals must negotiate choosing between (or negotiating) their own cultural value system and that proffered by the dominant society. Phinney et al. (1990) maintain that the way in which minority adolescents deal with and come to accept their status as minority members who face prejudice and who must negotiate a bicultural value system, impacts their sense of ethnic identity. Those adolescents who actively explore and resolve these struggles develop an achieved ethnic identity, whereas those who fail to do so develop a diffused or foreclosed identity.

Integrating the work of Tajfel (1978), Berry and Kim (1988), and others, Phinney et al. (1990) posit four possible coping outcomes that minority-status individuals use to deal with ethnic identity conflicts. *Alienation/ Marginalization* describes individuals who accept the negative self-image presented by society, become alienated from their own racial/ethnic cultural group, and do not adapt to the majority culture. *Assimilation* describes those individuals who attempt to become part of the dominant culture and do not maintain ties with their own racial/ethnic cultural group. *Withdrawal or Separation* describes individuals who emphasize their own culture and withdraw from contact with the majority or dominant group. Finally, *Integration/Biculturalism* describes those individuals who retain their ethnic culture and also adapt to the dominant culture by learning the necessary skills to succeed in the culture. There is some evidence that this integration stage is the most psychological healthy in terms of traditional measures of mental health such as high self-esteem and lower levels of anxiety and stress. More will be said about this research later in the chapter.

Phinney and her colleagues (Phinney, 1989; Phinney & Alipuria, 1990; Phinney et al., 1990; Phinney & Tarver, 1988) have presented an ethnic identity development model consistent with Marcia's (1966) ego identity model. Phinney's model has three distinct stages—*Diffusion/Foreclosure, Moratorium,* and *Achievement*—that elucidate the process by which minority adolescents explore ethnic issues and achieve a positive sense of themselves as minority group members.

Ethnic Identity Diffusion/Foreclosure

In the initial stage of ethnic identity development, the adolescent has not yet explored feelings/attitudes about his or her ethnicity. The adolescent may lack interest in the topic or see it as a nonissue (diffusion), or she or he may have attitudes about ethnicity derived from significant others carried over from childhood (foreclosure). Phinney et al. (1990) note that some minority adolescents in this stage may accept the values and attitudes of the dominant culture toward their group. These youth are at risk of internalizing negative stereotypes about their own group and expressing preferences for the dominant group. The majority of individuals at this stage, however, do not express preferences for the dominant group. Instead, they simply appear to be unconcerned about ethnicity and/or may not have given the topic of their ethnicity much thought.

Table 4.1 outlines the link and cross-over between Phinney's stage conceptualization with that of Marcia and other ethnic-identity theorists.

Table 4.1 Models of Racial/Ethnic Identity Development, Psychological Adjustment, and Prejudice

Models	Stage of Models					
General Identity Model						
Marcia (1981)	Identity Diffusion	Foreclosed Identity	Moratorium	Achieved Identity		
Minority Identity Models						
Phinney, Lochner, & Murphy (1990)	Diffusion/Foreclosure		Search/Moratorium	Achievement		
Atkinson, Morten, & Sue (1989)	Conformity	Dissonance	Resistance & Denial	Introspection	Synergetic Articulation	
Culture Specific Identity Models						
Cross (1991)	Pre-encounter	Encounter	Immersion/Emersion	Internalization		Internalization Commitment
Kim (1981)	White Identification / Ethnic Awareness	Awakening	Redirection	Incorporation		
Arce (1981)	Forced Identification	Internal Quest	Acceptance	Internalized		
Ponterotto & Pedersen Integrative Model	Identification with the White Majority	Awareness, Encounter and Search	Identification and Immersion	Integration and Internalization		
Psychological Adjustment	Negative	Mixed	Negative	Positive		
Prejudicial Inclinations of Various Identity Stages	Negative prejudice towards own group; positive prejudice toward white majority; potential of racism toward own group	Beginning positive prejudice toward own group and negative prejudice toward whites; some potential of racism toward whites	Positive prejudice toward own group; negative prejudice toward whites; potential of racism toward whites	Prejudice free; racism toward any group is highly unlikely		

The last two rows of Table 4.1 summarize the researched mental health correlates to the stages, as well as our hypothesized prejudicial dispositions associated with each stage.

Ethnic Identity Search/Moratorium

The second stage is characterized by an increasing awareness and exploration of ethnic identity issues. This newfound awareness is sometimes precipitated by a sudden experience or encounter that causes the adolescent to pause and consider the meaning of his or her ethnic background. The encounter may be blunt, like an experience with overt racism, or it may be more subtle, involving a number of less dramatic experiences that cause the adolescent to acknowledge that he or she is perceived (by the dominant group) as unequal by virtue of racial/ethnic affiliation. This awareness leads to an ethnic identity search (moratorium), whereby the adolescent attempts both to clarify the personal implications of race/ethnicity and learn more about her or his racial/ethnic group. This stage, as well as parallel stages in other models (see Table 4.1), is often characterized by emotional intensity. Individuals may experience anger and outrage toward the dominant White society; guilt, embarrassment, and self-directed anger may result from an acknowledgment of past naivete with regard to racial/ethnic issues.

Ethnic Identity Achievement

In the final stage of adolescent identity development, the individual has come to terms with racial/ethnic issues and has accepted herself or himself as a member of a minority group. The intense emotions characteristic of the previous stage have moderated. The individual has a calm, secure demeanor with regard to her or his cultural group, and is, at the same time, open to experiences outside the culture. In essence, a healthy bicultural identity is developed.

Atkinson, Morten, and Sue's Minority
Identity Development (MID) Model

Atkinson et al.'s (1989, 1993) MID model is anchored in the belief that all minority groups experience the common force of *oppression,* and, as a result, all will generate attitudes and behaviors consistent with a natural internal struggle to develop a strong sense of self- and group-identity in spite of oppressive conditions (see Smith, 1991, for a nonoppression-focused majority-minority identity model). The MID model is presented as a stage theory; however, the authors caution that the model is best conceptualized as a continuous process in which the stages blend into one another without clear or abrupt demarcations.

Each stage in the MID model is defined with respect to four attitudinal groupings: (a) attitudes toward oneself, (b) attitudes toward others in the same reference group, (c) attitudes toward members of other minority groups, and (d) attitudes toward the White majority group. The five stages are briefly described below.

Conformity

Minority individuals in Stage 1, Conformity, have an unequivocal preference for the values and norms of the dominant culture. They have a strong desire to assimilate and acculturate into the dominant culture. Individuals in this stage have negative, self-deprecating attitudes toward themselves as racial beings, as well as toward their racial group in general. Their view of other minority groups is dependent on how the dominant culture evaluates the groups. Conformity stage attitudes toward the dominant group are positive.

Dissonance

The Dissonance stage marks that point when minority individuals begin to question their Conformity, pro-White attitudes. Movement into the Dissonance stage is a gradual process, often stimulated by a personal race-related experience. For example, an individual who has been denying her or his racial/ethnic heritage (i.e., displaying Conformity attitudes) may meet and be strongly influenced by another member of her or his cultural group who displays ethnic pride and a cultural connection. Other Conformity individuals reach the Dissonance stage after a personal experience with racism. The Dissonance Stage is one of transition, and the individual is straddling both self- and group-appreciating and depreciating attitudes. Similarly, attitudes toward other minority groups and the majority group represent a mixture of both positive and negative attitudes. The Dissonance individual is in a state of flux and confusion.

Resistance and Immersion

At Stage 3, Resistance and Immersion, the minority individual comes to embrace his or her own racial/ethnic group completely. This stage is characterized by a blanket endorsement of one's group and all the values and attitudes attributed to the group. At the same time there is a rejection of the values and norms associated with the dominant group. The individual has now completely broken through the denial characteristic of the Conformity stage and questioned in the Dissonance stage, and now accepts racism and oppression as a reality. Resistance attitudes are associated with guilt over previously held [and now believed to be naive] Conformity attitudes. Anger, even rage, is experienced now as the individual contemplates his or her role as an oppressed member of society. Attitudes toward the dominant group in Resistance and Immersion are very negative, while attitudes toward self and members of the same racial/ethnic group are unequivocally positive. Resistance stage attitudes toward members of other minority groups are conflictual, characterized simultaneously by an empathic understanding and an overpowering ethnocentric bias.

Introspection

During Introspection, the rigid ethnocentric views of the previous stage begin to attenuate. There is a comfort and security in one's racial identity that allows the questioning of rigid Resistance attitudes. There is a feeling that much of the anger and negativity previously directed toward the "White system" could be better used in the positive exploration of identity issues. During this stage, the minority individual feels concern with regard to the basis of self- and group-appreciating attitudes. There is some conflict between one's allegiance to his or her ethnic group and issues of personal autonomy. Views toward one's racial/ethnic group are now not blindly positive, and individual differentiation is considered. Attitudes toward the dominant group are also conflictual. Although there is still distrust of the "system" to some degree, individual variation is acknowledged (e.g., not all White people are racist).

Synergetic Articulation and Awareness

This final stage of the MID model is characterized by a sense of self-fulfillment with regard to cultural identity. The individual has a confident and secure racial identity, and there is a desire to eliminate all forms of oppression, not just oppression aimed at one's own group. Synergetic attitudes reflect a generally high level of positive regard toward self and toward one's group. Unlike the Resistance and Immersion Stage, however, the Synergetic stage is not characterized by a blanket acceptance of all values and norms of the group. Racial group membership constitutes just one important facet of the person's life, and there is a high level of personal autonomy. Synergetic attitudes toward other minority groups are positive. There is respect and appreciation of other cultural groups as well as acknowledgment that other minority groups in America have their own unique history of oppression. Finally, Synergetic attitudes toward the dominant group are characterized by selective appreciation. The individual is receptive to dominant culture persons who themselves seek a halt to minority-group oppression, and there is an openness to constructive elements of the dominant culture.

Culture-Specific Models of Racial/Ethnic Identity Development

The adolescent model of Phinney et al. (1990) and the adult model of Atkinson et al. (1989) are relatively recent developments. These models, to a large degree, have been extensions and integrations of longer standing, more fully researched culture- or race-specific models. This section of Chapter 4 reviews three such models covering the following groups: African Americans (Cross, 1991), Asian Americans (more specifically Japanese Americans; Kim, 1981), and Mexican Americans (Arce, 1981). Of all the racial or ethnic identity models, Cross's model has received the most conceptual attention and empirical scrutiny. It is also the longest-standing model of those we have chosen to review, and, therefore, we begin our discussion with it.

Cross's Model of Black Identity Development

William E. Cross, Jr. is a leading theorist in the area of Black racial identity development (see also the influential work of Thomas, 1971). His initial explication (Cross, 1971) of the "Negro-to-Black Conversion Experience" appeared in the journal *Black World*; it has been cited as one of the most referenced conceptual documents in the counseling literature (see Ponterotto & Sabnani, 1989). Cross has continued to flesh out his theory during two decades of research on the model (see Cross, 1978, 1987, 1989, 1991; Cross, Parham, & Helms, in press; Helms, 1990b; Parham, 1989). Cross's model focuses on *Nigrescence,* the "process of becoming Black" (Cross, 1991, p. 157). Helms (1990a, p. 17) defines Nigrescence as ". . . the developmental process by which a person 'becomes Black' where Black is defined in terms of one's manner of thinking about and evaluating oneself and one's reference groups rather than in terms of skin color per se. Cross (1991, p. 190) notes that nigrescence "... is a model that explains how *assimilated* Black adults, as well as *deracinated, deculturalized* or *miseducated* Black adults are transformed by a series of circumstances and events into persons who are more Black or Afrocentrically aligned." Cross (1991) describes five stages: (a) Pre-encounter is stage one, and it depicts the identity to be changed; (b) stage two, Encounter, isolates the point at which the individual feels compelled to change; (c) Immersion-Emersion is stage three and describes the vortex of identity change; and (d) stages four and five, Internalization and Internalization-Commitment, describe the internalization of the new identity.

Pre-encounter

Nigrescence is a resocializing experience that transforms a pre-existing non-Afrocentric identity to an identity that is Afrocentric. Pre-encounter describes the pre-existing identity. Pre-encounter attitudes can vary along a continuum from low salience to anti-Black. Individuals with low salience views do not place much significance on being Black. They do not deny being Black, but see this "physical" characteristic as unrelated to their sense of happiness and well-being. These individuals may put more value (have higher salience) on other identity aspects such as religion, social status, profession, or life style. Cross (1991) also notes that "some low-salience types simply have not given much thought to race issues; they seem to be dumbfounded and naive during racial discussions" (p. 191).

Other low-salience individuals have given some thought to being Black but focus on race as a problem or stigma. They tie race to issues of social discrimination and, therefore, perceive race as a hassle that has to be dealt with. On the other end of the salience continuum are those Blacks who see being Black as very important, but in a negative way. These individuals are anti-Black, feel alienated from other Blacks, and do not see the Black community as a potential or actual source of personal support. It was this aspect of Pre-encounter attitudes that was the focus of Cross's (1971) early theorizing, as well as much of the counseling research on the Pre-encounter stage (see Helms, 1989, 1990b; Ponterotto & Wise, 1987).

According to Cross (1991), the Pre-encounter identity is the person's first identity to be shaped by early development: socialization in the family, neighborhood, community, and schools. It begins in childhood and extends through adolescence and early adulthood. Stage two of the model, Encounter, pinpoints those circumstances and events that are likely to induce identity reconsideration in the individual.

Encounter

Cross emphasizes that because a person's current level of identity is resistant to change, an encounter of some form must catch the person "off guard." Specifically, Cross (1991, p. 199) states, "The encounter must work around, slip through, or even shatter the relevance of the person's current identity and world view, and at the same time provide some hint of the direction in which to point the person to be resocialized or transformed."

At times, this critical encounter can be a single event, such as being confronted personally with racism. A dramatic event that sent many Pre-encounter Blacks searching for a deeper understanding of Afrocentricity was the assassination of Dr. Martin Luther King, Jr. In some instances, the encounter is not a single event but a series of small, eye-opening episodes that erode the individual's Pre-encounter identity. These small episodes have a cumulative effect, and at a certain point the person experiences a strong push toward nigrescence.

Cross highlights that the Encounter stage is a two-stage process: the person must experience an encounter *and* personalize it. For example, "in April 1968, not every Black person who heard about the death of Dr. Martin Luther King, Jr. was transformed into a Black Power advocate. Some people 'experienced' the event, but it did not lead to change" (Cross, 1991, p. 200). Others, however, were personally traumatized by Dr. King's death, and it called into question their embracement of integrationist views.

Finally, it is important to note that the encounter experience may not necessarily be negative. For example, individuals may be exposed to historical information about the Black experience that they were previously unfamiliar with. Giving credence to and personalizing this information may lead to identity change. Regardless of the context of the encounter experience, however, the individual inevitably "becomes enraged at the thought of having been previously miseducated by White racist institutions" (Cross, 1991, p. 200). The Encounter stage engenders a great range of emotions. Initially there may be alarm, confusion, and depression; guilt may set in as the individuals acknowledge how naive they were about racial issues; and an emerging anxiety and anger often develops.

Immersion-Emersion

Cross (1991) states that:

> The Immersion-Emersion stage of nigrescence addresses the most sensational aspect of Black identity development, for it represents the vortex of psychological nigrescence. . . . During this period of transition, the person begins to demolish the old perspective and simultaneously tries to construct what will become his or her new frame of reference. (pp. 201-202)

The Immersion-Emersion individual has now decided to commit to a transformed identity, but she or he is more familiar with the old identity than with the new identity. This sets the stage for a frantic identity search. Cross (1991) describes both the Immersion and Emersion steps of this transitional period.

Immersion describes the first step of this stage and portrays an individual who immerses himself or herself into an Afrocentric world. This person becomes active both politically and socially in the Black cause. There is a positive association with anything Black and a concurrent negative association with anything White. There is a strong anti-White sentiment at this point. In relationships with other Blacks, the Immersion individual is assessing and evaluating their "level of Blackness," what Cross (1991, p. 203) terms the "Blacker-than-thou" syndrome. Cross (1991) highlights the emotional intensity of this step as follows:

> This immersion is a strong, powerful, dominating sensation that is constantly energized by rage (at White people and culture), guilt (at having once been tricked into thinking Negro ideas), and a developing sense of pride (in one's Black self, in Black people, and in Black culture.) (p. 203)

The second phase of this stage, Emersion, describes individuals who come to the conclusion that their immersed impressions of Blackness were romanticized and exaggerated. The individual begins now to demonstrate a "more serious" understanding of Black issues. Cross (1991) describes this Emersion as

> an emergence from the emotionality and dead-end, either-or, racist and oversimplified ideologies of the immersion experience. The person regains control of his or her emotions and intellect. In fact, he or she probably cannot continue to handle the intense emotional phase [of immersion] and is predisposed to find a way to level off. (p. 207)

Internalization

The Internalization stage marks the period when a new identity is incorporated. The person now feels more relaxed, calmer, and more at ease with himself or herself. An inner peace is achieved, as there has been a shift

> from uncontrolled rage toward White people to controlled anger at oppressive systems and racist institutions; from symbolic, boisterous rhetoric to serious analysis and 'quiet' strength; . . . from anxious, insecure, rigid pseudo-Blackness based on the hatred of Whites to proactive Black pride, self-love, and a deep sense of connection to, and acceptance by, the Black community (Cross, 1991, p. 210).

The internalized individual is secure in his or her Blackness and, at the same time, is open to new experiences. In effect, the individual's own internal security and comfort with his or her racial identity nourishes any experimentation with new experiences. Such an individual may become bicultural or even multicultural in orientation. A multicultural orientation to life in a heterogeneous, culturally diverse society is considered an ideal and most healthy perspective on human relationships (see the extensive work of Ramirez, 1991).

Cross (1991) highlights that psychological nigrescence does not transform one's personality. Although the emotional roller-coaster ride that characterizes Immersion-Emersion does stress the individual, once the new identity is internalized there is a reduction of psychological stress. Therefore, a shy person at Pre-encounter is still a shy person at Internalization; a nervous and anxious person at Pre-encounter remains nervous and anxious at Internalization, and a happy Pre-encounter person is also happy at Internalization.

Internalization-Commitment

The key marker of the Internalization-Commitment stage is a sustained, long-term commitment to activity in Black issues. Not all internalized individuals sustain a long-term interest in Black affairs; those that do, are in this final stage. Cross (1991) points out that the psychology of Blacks at this and the previous stage is similar in most ways, with sustained commitment being the distinguishing factor. Therefore, many of the descriptions in the Internalization stage apply also to this final stage.

Kim's Model of Asian-American Identity Development

Kim (1981) conducted an exploratory study to "examine the process by which Asian Americans resolve their identity conflict around being Americans of Asian ancestry, living in a predominantly White society" (p. vi). Kim's sample consisted of ten Sansei (third generation) Japanese-American women. Kim's retrospective results indicate that identity conflict is resolved through a developmental, progressive, and sequential process. This process involves five stages; progressing through them moves the individual from a state of negative self-concept and identity conflict to one of positive self-concept and a positive identification with Asian Americans. The five stages identified and described by Kim are Ethnic Awareness, White Identification, Awakening to Social Political Consciousness, Redirection to Asian-American Consciousness, and Incorporation.

Ethnic Awareness

This first stage occurs prior to entering elementary school, at around 3 or 4 years of age, when the individual first comes to know his or her ethnic origins. This awareness comes primarily through interactions with family members and relatives.

During these early childhood years, the attitudes of Kim's subjects towards being Japanese were either positive or neutral, depending on the extent of family involvement in ethnic activities. The children with greater exposure to Japanese culture and ethnic activities had a more positive self-concept and a more clear ego identity. The children with less exposure recalled having a more neutral self-concept and a confused ego-identity as Japanese Americans.

Stage 1 lasts until the children begin school. This developmental change—beginning school—brought the children into more frequent and often less hospitable contact with White society. For Kim's (1981) adult subjects who were thinking back to this time, this movement into the formal educational structure was invariably a negative one with regard to the effects of others' prejudice on their self-perception.

White Identification

Through increased contact with the White society, Asian-American children begin to develop a sense that they are different from their peers.

Feeling different was primarily the result of negative encounters with other children's racial prejudices. The children were not prepared for this and responded by personalizing their situation, leading them to believe it was their fault. Invariably, the subjects in Kim's study remembered this period as a painful experience, a time when their self-concept became negative.

Being treated as different and inferior led Kim's subjects to identify with White people. They began to internalize White societal values, and become alienated from self and from other Asian Americans. Kim (1981, p. 129) notes that

> During this stage all subjects have subconsciously internalized overt, positive, White images, especially regarding standards of physical beauty and attractiveness. Hence, alienation from oneself is experienced primarily as a negative self-image focused around physical attributes.

Buying into White society's view that Asian Americans are less attractive, Kim's (1981) subjects were not very involved in dating during adolescence and instead focused their energy towards involvement in formal organizational roles (e.g., class president, club leaders, yearbook editor, etc.) and in academic pursuits.

The extent of "White identification" during this stage varied among the subjects. Some identified *actively,* considering themselves as very similar to White peers and not consciously acknowledging cultural differences. These subjects saw themselves as White and acted accordingly. They did not want to be seen as Asian in any way. In contrast, during *passive* White identification, subjects did not consider themselves as White, although they did accept as a reference point, White standards, values, and beliefs.

Interestingly, Kim points out that those subjects who experienced the "Ethnic Awareness" stage as neutral (those whose families were not very involved in Japanese ethnic culture and activities) were more likely to actively identity with Whites, whereas those subjects whose "Ethnic Awareness" stage was more culturally involved, were more likely to identify only passively with Whites and White cultural norms.

Awakening to Social Political Consciousness

During this stage, individuals develop a new perspective of who they are in society. This perspective involves seeing oneself as a minority in society. Often a significant event (e.g., moving to the west coast and having increased contact with politically conscious Asian Americans) initiates the awakening to political consciousness. Kim's subjects' "awakening" was stimulated and activated by the social environment—e.g., the civil rights and women's movements of the 1960s and 1970s, or by politically active family members, partners, or friends.

At this stage, subjects shed their previously White-identified values and reassess the merits of White standards. This reassessment sometimes leads to political alienation from White society. Now the subjects' reference group centers on political and social philosophy. Their ego identity is now "centered around being a minority, being oppressed, not being inferior, and feeling connected to experiences of other minorities" (Kim, 1981, pp. 144-145). It is during this stage that self-concept becomes more positive.

Redirection to Asian-American Consciousness

In the preceding stage Kim's subjects had changed their identification from White-oriented to minority-oriented. In the Redirection stage individuals begin to embrace their Asian-American identity. Their political/ social involvement in the previous stage bolstered their self-concept, and now they desire to embrace their own racial/ethnic identity and immerse themselves in the Asian American heritage.

During this immersion period subjects can feel very angry and outraged at White society. They realize that White racism was the foundation for their negative experiences and for their previous identification with White standards and values. In time, individuals in this stage are able to work through this emotionally laden reactionary phase and come to a realistic reappraisal of both themselves and other Asian Americans. In this redirection stage, self-concept is positive, and individuals feel good about themselves and proud to be Asian American.

Incorporation

In the final stage of Asian-American identity development put forth by Kim (1981), individuals come to a healthy and secure balance, feeling comfortable with their own identity yet appreciative of other racial groups. Individuals at this stage do not feel the driving need to either identify with or against White people. They develop a realistic appraisal of all people. Asian-American identity is important but only one aspect of their overall identity. There is a healthy blending of racial/ethnic identity with other identities central to the individual's overall view of self and self-concept (e.g., religious identity, political ideology, sexual and sex role orientation, and career/professional identity).

Arce's Model of Chicano Identity

Arce (1981) reviews the literature on group consciousness processes for Chicanos and describes a transition where people stop thinking of themselves as Mexican American and begin to see themselves as Chicano. Reaching *Chicanismo* involves two forms of self-awareness: (a) political awareness, which is the knowledge of the Mexican people's history in the United States and an awareness of the effects of discrimination on the group; and (b) cultural awareness, which is manifested in pride in one's language and cultural values.

Arce (1981) does not name specific stages in the ethnic identity process as do other theorists (e.g., Cross, 1991; Kim, 1981), yet his transitional descriptions, in many ways, closely parallel other identity models reviewed previously in this chapter. For ease of cross-reference to other stage models, we have given names to Arce's stage process. Arce's model can be organized into four stages: Forced Identification, Internal Quest, Acceptance, and Internalized Ethnic Identity. The context for this identity model stems from the experiences of Mexican-American students studying in a health sciences program.

During *Forced Identification,* students are identified as Hispanic or Mexican American by others, often by school officials who need to document affirmative action data. According to Arce (1981, p. 185), some individuals "disavow the identification by muting ethnic characteristics or by reconstructing their personal histories." Some individuals may acquiesce to this forced ethnic identification and then find that it stimulates an *Internal Quest* for one's cultural roots. This leads to an *Acceptance* of one's group which is characterized by group loyalty and pride. Finally, the acceptance of and pride in one's group leads to an *Internalized Ethnic Identity.* This final stage is characterized by a deep sense of belonging to one's cultural group, by a desire to be accepted by the group, and by a desire to do something for the group. Arce (1981) states that in this final stage

> Associational preferences shift inward, particularly toward people who will reciprocate the new identity. A strong, new kinship develops with all Chicanos, and individual personal commitments include action in behalf of the group. When the person finally comes to feel at one with the group, the internalization process has been completed, and ethnic identity established. (p. 186)

Arce further notes that the identity process is generally directional, but it is not fully linear, as students may go back and forth between points on the stage continuum.

Integration of Identity Models and Relationship to Mental Health and Prejudice

As you read through the different racial/ethnic identity models you probably noticed that there are many commonalities that transcend the various models. As there are similarities, there are also some unique aspects to individual models. For example, Kim's (1981) first stage, *Ethnic Awareness,* has no direct parallel in the other models. This stage begins in early childhood, whereas the first stage in the other models take place in adolescence or young adulthood. Another unique stage is the *Internalization-Commitment* stage of the Cross (1991) model. This stage represents an advanced commitment to social causes and is characterized by a life's devotion to work on racial justice. Only the Cross model extends racial identity development to this level.

This concluding section of Chapter 4 highlights the mental health correlates of diverse stages. Furthermore, we hypothesize about unresearched links between ethnic identity development and dispositions toward prejudice.

Although the models differ with respect to the number of stages or phases represented in the process of racial/ethnic identity development, common themes can be extracted. Collapsing stages across the five different identity models reveals the four transcendent themes (or stages) below.

Identification With the White Majority

Many of the models posit a point where minority individuals identify primarily with the White majority culture. The degree or intensity of this identification can vary. In Phinney et al.'s (1990) Diffusion/Foreclosure stage, the adolescent may simply lack interest in the race/ethnicity concept and not see it as relevant to his or her life. In other models there may be a more active identification with Whites and even a disavowal of one's own racial or ethnic group. In Cross's (1991) Pre-encounter stage and Atkinson et al.'s (1989) Conformity stage, there is an unequivocal preference for dominant cultural values. Kim's (1981) White-Identified stage and Arce's (1981) Forced Identification stage also posit a preference for the standards, norms, and values of the dominant White culture.

Generally, research on this phase of identity development has pointed to a negative correlation with positive mental health indices. Phinney (1989) found that 10th grade Black, Mexican-American, and Asian-American adolescents in her Diffusion/Foreclosure stage scored lower on four levels of psychological adjustment: self evaluation, sense of mastery, social and peer relations, and family relations. Focusing on Black, Asian-American, and Mexican-American college students, Phinney and Alipuria (1990) found stage 1 students to have lower self esteem (see reviews in Phinney, 1990; Phinney et al., 1990).

The majority of mental health research on this stage has focused on Cross's model and has incorporated the Racial Identity Attitude Scale (RIAS; Helms, 1990c; Helms & Parham, 1990; Parham & Helms, 1981) as the measurement device. Both Parham and Helms (1985a) and Nottingham, Rosen, and Parks (1992) found Black college students in this early phase (Pre-encounter) to have lower self esteem. In a related article, Parham and Helms (1985b) found Pre-encounter attitudes to be positively related to feelings of inferiority and anxiety. Carter (1991) examined the relationship of Black racial identity to measures of psychological well-being on the Bell Global Psychopathology Scale. He found Pre-encounter attitudes positively related to higher levels of anxiety, memory impairment, paranoia, hallucinations, and alcohol concerns.

Focusing on women college students, Pyant and Yanico (1991) found Pre-encounter attitudes predictive of lower self-esteem and a lower sense of well-being among African-American women (college) students and nonstudents. These authors also found that with African-American nonstudent women, Pre-encounter attitudes were positively related to depression. Taub and McEwen (1992) found high Pre-encounter attitudes in Black college women correlated to lower levels of autonomy, academic autonomy, and mature interpersonal relationships.

In a study of Black college students' participation in campus cultural and noncultural organizations, Mitchell and Dell (1992) found Pre-encounter attitudes were inversely related to participation in culturally related campus organizations.

In terms of the relationship between Stage 1 individuals and dispositions toward prejudice, we would predict negative prejudice towards one's own racial/ethnic group and a positive prejudice toward the White dominant culture. These individuals are clearly more in danger of being racist toward their own group than toward White persons.

Awareness, Encounter, and Search

The second stage of our four-stage integrative model is characterized by an examination and questioning of previously held White-preference attitudes. Minority adolescents and adults begin to question their status as minorities in a racist society, and they begin a search for their own racial/ethnic identity. This search can be stimulated by a single blunt encounter with an oppressive or racist experience or by an accumulation of more subtle experiences. All five identity models have stages that fit into this integrative stage: Phinney et al.'s (1990) Search/Moratorium, Atkinson et al.'s (1989) Dissonance, Cross's (1991) Encounter, Kim's (1981) Awakening to Social Political Consciousness, and Arce's (1981) Internal Quest. Interestingly, many of the identity theorists note how this stage is accompanied by feelings of confusion, anger, and even embarrassment.

The second stage of our integrative model has been associated with both positive and negative mental health indices. The empirical research in this stage was also based on Cross's model and utilized the Racial Identity Attitude Scale to measure the respective stages. Parham and Helms (1985a) found high self-esteem associated with Cross's Encounter stage. Mitchell and Dell (1992) found Encounter attitudes positively related to participation in campus cultural organizations. On the other hand, Pyant and Yanico (1991) found Encounter attitudes among (nonstudent) African-American women to be associated with higher levels of depression and lower levels of self-esteem and psychological well-being. Furthermore, Taub and McEwen (1992) found high Encounter attitudes among Black college women to be correlated to lower levels of academic autonomy, mature interpersonal relationships, and intimacy.

Other researchers have found no significant relationship between the Encounter stage and measures of psychological health (e.g., Carter, 1991; Nottingham et al., 1992). It is clear that more focused research is needed in this area. One avenue for investigation would be to examine the contradictory findings of the studies by looking closely at differences in sample characteristics and in the mental health assessment measures employed by the respective researchers.

Given the empirical findings and theoretical formulations of this stage, we would hypothesize that confusion about one's own racial group and other racial groups is most salient at this point. Individuals at this stage may be beginning to develop positive prejudice toward their own racial group and a concurrent negative prejudice toward the White majority. We would expect individuals in Stage 2 to be confused about allegiances with members of other minority groups. They would be weary of the "White system," and looking to connect and align themselves with their own racial/ethnic group. Very likely, individuals in Stage Two are developing racial/ethnic prejudices, but they are not formed well enough to be transformed into actual racist behavior.

Identification and Immersion

Stage 3 of our integrative model depicts individuals who have searched for their own identity (a process began in Stage 2) and are now committing and immersing themselves in their own racial/ethnic cultural roots. Stage 3 individuals are likely to completely endorse the norms/values and customs of their own group, while at the same time completely rejecting values or norms associated with the White establishment. Phinney et al.'s (1990) Search/Moratorium has aspects of this stage as does Atkinson et al.'s (1989) Resistance and Denial stage, the Immersion portion of Cross's (1991) Immersion-Emersion stage, Kim's (1981) Redirection to Asian-American Consciousness stage, and, to some degree, Arce's (1981) Acceptance stage.

An important component of Stage 3 is its intense emotionality. Often anger and rage are directed at the White majority, concurrent with an almost idealized and romanticized view of one's own racial/ethnic group. With regard to mental health research, Parham and Helms (1985a) found lower self-esteem associated with Immersion attitudes; their related study (Parham & Helms, 1985b) found higher levels of anxiety and inferiority associated with Immersion attitudes. Taub and McEwen (1992) found high Immersion attitudes correlated to lower levels of intimacy, academic autonomy, and mature interpersonal relationships. Carter (1991) found Immersion attitudes predictive of self-reported concerns about drug use. This study also found this stage associated with fewer memory difficulties. Finally, Mitchell and Dell (1992) found Immersion attitudes positively correlated to participation in cultural campus organizations.

Individuals in Stage 3, Identification and Immersion, are likely to have a high level of positive prejudice toward their own racial/ethnic group coupled with a high level of negative prejudice toward the White majority group. These individuals are more likely to act in a racist way toward Whites than individuals in the previous stage.

Integration and Internalization

One commonality among the stage models is that after a period of intense identification or immersion in one's own culture, there is a reassessment and reappraisal out of which a more balanced bicultural identity develops. Atkinson et al.'s (1989) Introspection stage, and the Emersion portion of Cross's (1991) Immersion-Emersion stage specifically describe this reappraisal attitude. Also, the intense emotion of the previous phase—negative toward Whites and positive towards one's own group—becomes attenuated in this final stage, the major characteristic of which is the development of a secure racial/ethnic identity coupled with an appreciation of other cultures. In essence, a bicultural or multicultural identity development is established (this multicultural identity is similar to the multicultural personality construct described by Ramirez [1991]). Phinney et al.'s (1990) Achievement stage, Atkinson et al.'s (1989) Synergetic Articulation and Awareness stage, Cross's (1991) Internalization, Kim's (1981) Incorporation, and Arce's (1981) Internalized stage all fall under our fourth and final stage.

Some research has associated Stage 4 attitudes with positive mental health indices. Phinney's (1989; Phinney & Alipuria, 1990) research, cited earlier, found that minority adolescents in an Achieved Identity status scored highest on measures of self-esteem and psychological adjustment. Using the Cross model, Nottingham et al. (1992) found Internalization attitudes positively related to self-esteem. However, Parham and Helms (1985a) did not find this same relationship, and in their related study (Parham & Helms, 1985b) they did not find Internalization attitudes to be significantly related to self-actualizing tendencies. Furthermore, Taub and McEwen (1992) found no significant correlations between Internalization attitudes and measures of psychosocial development (namely levels of autonomy and mature interpersonal relationships).

Mitchell and Dell (1992) did find Cross's Internalization stage to be significantly and positively related to participation in both cultural and noncultural campus organizations. This finding supports the notion of a student with well-balanced campus involvements. Finally, Carter (1991) found Internalization attitudes predictive of higher levels of paranoia. However, Carter (1991) notes that as a result of the bicultural skill and awareness associated with this stage that hypersensitivity (or cultural paranoia) may serve a healthy adaptive purpose.

Chapter Summary

This chapter reviewed models of minority identity development in the context of the identity development work of Erikson (1950, 1968) and Marcia (1980). General minority adolescent and adult models were discussed as were race/ethnic-specific models applicable to African Americans, Asian Americans, and Mexican Americans.

The limited research associating identity stages to mental health indices was reviewed. Although there appear to be some trends in this research, the quantity of such research is too limited to arrive at any definitive conclusions. Furthermore, the research is overdependent on Helms's (1990b) Black and White Racial Identity scales, which are not without limitations (see reviews in Alexander, 1992; Sabnani & Ponterotto, 1992).

This chapter also hypothesized probable relationships between diverse identity stages and one's likelihood to be prejudiced toward both the White majority and one's own racial/ethnic group. A major point of this chapter is that developing a healthy racial/ethnic identity is a central component of one's overall self-concept. Furthermore, appreciation and respect of other racial/ethnic groups may not be very likely if one does not feel good about one's own racial/ethnic group. Consequently, an important emphasis that needs to be included in prejudice prevention programming is that of developing a healthy and positive racial/ethnic identity.

Chapter 5 parallels Chapter 4 in format and covers models of majority (or White) identity development. The relationship of White identity development to racism is highlighted. Chapter 6 then examines the role of the counselor in promoting healthy racial/ethnic identity development.

5

White Racial Identity Development and Prejudice Prevention

Counselors and educators for years have considered the feelings that minority clients and students hold toward themselves and toward the White majority. Common questions examined by counselors include: "How does this minority client/student feel about being in a minority"? "Is this client comfortable interacting with Whites"? "Does the client trust White people"? "Is the client proud of or embarrassed by his or her racial/ethnic affiliation"? In summary, minority clients and students traditionally have been the focus of racial identity consideration, whereas counselors and educators, the majority of whom are White, have not been led to examine their own comfort with racial issues.

This chapter focuses on White racial identity development and examines the process Whites in America undergo in acknowledging their race and accepting the social implications of their racial group membership—power, privilege, and responsibility for change. Theory and research in the last ten years on White racial identity development leads us to conclude that the topic is of such importance that it should be a focus of education in general, and of counseling training in particular.

The purpose of this chapter is to review leading theories of White racial identity development and to examine the relationship of this development to prejudice and racism. As we noted in Chapter 4, facilitating interracial harmony begins with the long-term process of exploring and coming to terms with one's own racial identity. The first theorist to put forth a well articulated model of White racial identity development was Rita Hardiman. Hardiman's (1982) doctoral dissertation study was the basis for the model.

Hardiman's Generic Stages of Social Identity Development

Hardiman (1982) examines the constructs of racial identity and sex-role identity within the broader conception of what she terms "social identity." Building from the work of sociologists (e.g., Dashfsky, 1976), anthropologists (e.g., Robbins, 1973), and psychologists (e.g., Erikson, 1968; Tajfel, 1974), Hardiman developed a model of social identity consisting of five stages. She defines social identity as ". . . all the various social groups that an individual consciously or unconsciously has membership in and the conscious or unconscious use of that social frame of reference in self-perception, in social perception or in social interaction" (Hardiman, 1982, p. 76). Hardiman's (1982) often-cited model of White Racial Identity represents one aspect of social identity. Other aspects of social identity include sex-role identity, occupational identity, and religious identity. Before we examine Hardiman's White Identity model, it is important to review her broader social identity model.

Hardiman examined and integrated available racial/ethnic identity models (Cross, 1971; Hayes-Bautista, 1974; Jackson, 1976; Kim, 1981; Thomas, 1971) and sex-role identity theories (Block, 1973; Pleck, 1976; Rebecca, Hefner, & Oleshansky, 1976) to arrive at a five-stage generic model of social identity development that would subsequently form the foundation of her White Identity model. The five stages are: No Social Consciousness, Acceptance, Resistance, Redefinition, and Internalization.

No Social Consciousness

This stage is characterized by spontaneous, natural behavior with regard to one's social attitudes or behavior. Individuals in this stage are unaware of or confused about their expected social role. Pressures to conform to particular social norms and behaviors have not yet been internalized.

Acceptance

Stage 2 is characterized by identification with role models and imitation or modelling of behavior. At this point stereotypes are developed and rigidly adhered to. The individual in Acceptance conforms to social expectations of appropriate behavior as a member of a particular social group (be it racial group, gender group, etc.). Stage 2 is also characterized by a rejection and devaluing of behaviors or characteristics that do not fit the social group's expectations.

Resistance

At Stage 3, the individual begins to question previously held beliefs about himself or herself as a member of a social group. Feelings of discomfort and anger emerge as one acknowledges his or her conformist attitude with regard to the social group. Stage 3 individuals begin to reject the social group's pressure to conform, and a new perspective or consciousness about the group is formed.

Redefinition

In Stage 4, individuals are introspective about their social group and begin to define their specific needs separate from the group as a whole. There is a rediscovery of and a renewed interest in one's heritage and culture as a member of the social group. This stage is characterized by pride and esteem in one's group membership.

Internalization

This final stage of social identity development involves the integration of aspects of identity achieved in the previous stage into the individual's overall social identity. The individual in Internalization is flexible, open-minded, and, to some degree, autonomous. There is interest and development in other aspects of one's social identity. The Stage 5 individual also displays empathy for individuals of the same social group who are at earlier stages of development.

With this brief overview of Hardiman's (1982) Social Identity Development Model in hand, we can now turn to a more extensive discussion of her White Identity Development Model. As noted earlier, the White

Identity model was developed in the context of the more general social identity theory.

Hardiman's White Identity Development Model (WID)

To examine White racial identity development in the context of social identity theory, Hardiman (1982) studied six autobiographies written by White authors describing their experiences and lives as White Americans. Each author (there were four women and two men, with various regions of the country represented) discussed her or his growth and development regarding racial issues and racism. The autobiographies selected were *Killers of the Dream* (Lillian Smith, 1963), *The Wall Between* (Anne Braden, 1958), *Confessional of a White Racist* (Larry King, 1971), *The Education of a WASP* (Lois Stalvey, 1970), *Hey, White Girl* (Susan Gregory, 1970), and *White on White: An Anti-Racism Manual for White Educators in the Process of Becoming* (James Edler, 1974). Hardiman's (1982) model consists of five stages, the names of which correspond to the social identity stage names listed previously.

Lack of Social Consciousness

Stage 1 individuals are unaware of the complex codes of appropriate behavior for White people. Individuals in this first stage naively operate from their own needs, interests and curiosity. As a result, they break many social rules and are chastised for their thoughts and actions. It is at this point that White people begin to learn what it means to be White and what other Whites consider appropriate attitudes and behaviors with regard to racial issues. Hardiman (1982, p. 158) cites the autobiography of Anne Braden (1958, p. 21) where the author recalls a childhood conversation with her mother. During the course of this conversation Anne happened to use the term "colored lady," to which her mom quickly retorted " 'You never call colored people ladies, Ann Gambrell [maiden name]' I can hear her voice now. 'You say colored women and white lady—never a colored lady.' " Stage 1 covers birth to about 4 or 5 years of age. The White authors recall this period as the time that awareness of racial differences began. Given the early-life period of this stage, the authors recalled the time as confusing. During this early stage, White children do not feel hostile, fearful, or superior to Blacks, but they may experience some discomfort in interracial situations. The authors also describe this period as one in which they were curious about racially diverse persons.

Acceptance

The transition to Stage 2, *Acceptance,* occurs as a result of socialization by parents, educators, peers, the church, the media, and the larger surrounding community (Hardiman, 1982). In the transition period, White children quickly learn the systematic ideology around race. They learn what shared opinions and behaviors [with regard to racial issues and interactions] are acceptable and unacceptable—which will be met with punishment and derision, and which will be met with glowing approval. This powerful socialization results in the staunch acceptance of behavior and beliefs that support the social codes. The dominant belief system becomes internalized, and no conscious effort is needed to remind the individual what thoughts or actions are socially appropriate. The prevailing unspoken attitude with regard to Black and White racial beliefs was captured in Braden's autobiography (Braden, 1958, pp. 19-21; cited in Hardiman, 1982, pp. 170-171).

It was most regrettable that the Negroes had ever been brought to this country in the first place and slavery had certainly been wrong. The presence of the Negroes in the South today was probably our punishment for the sins of our forefathers in bringing them here as slaves. . . . Negroes were really not bad creatures and certainly they had their uses, as they were available as domestic servants so white women could be freed of the burden of housework. . . . The point was to treat them kindly, not only because this was of course right according to Biblical teaching but also because if you treat a Negro with kindness he is also good to you—somewhat in the way a pet dog is good to the master who is good to him. And of course, the Negro people are happy in this relationship, there is not a reason to feel sorry for them—goodness, they are more carefree and there's nothing they like better than having some white folks who will take care of them.

Hardiman (1982) notes that unlike Stage 1, which is relatively brief in duration, Stage 2 can last many years, even a lifetime. Most of the autobiographies describe this stage in great detail, and many of the authors were in their adult years before encountering circumstances that would facilitate the transition to Stage 3.

Resistance

The transition from Stage 2 to Stage 3 is often a confusing and painful one. It is at this point that the White authors acknowledge the reality of the Black experience in America. The transition to Stage 3 is frequently stimulated by interaction with people, social events, or information presented in the media or in books. For example, King (1971, p. 17, cited in Hardiman, 1982, p. 180) found his *Acceptance* stage belief system challenged by reading a library book:

> I was a grown man before discovering that George Washington and Thomas Jefferson (those wise, saintly men whose pronouncements on liberty and justice leaped from my textbooks and echoed from the mouths of our Independence Day orators . . .) had owned slaves. It was shocking to learn that demigods who had influenced documents affirming the thrilling, limitless doctrine that *all men are created equal* had been otherwise capable of holding men in bondage for the profit from their sweat. I well remember discovering these new lessons in the Midland County Library, in my twentieth-first year, and then standing outside, looking up at the windswept streets, and thinking, "Hell, if they lied to me about *that*, they've lied to me about everything."

Hardiman notes that Whites experience painful emotions during the transition to Stage 3. These feelings range from guilt and embarrassment at having been foolish enough to believe the racist messages they received to anger and disgust at the system and people who lied to them. Stage 3 individuals acknowledge their whiteness and they understand that they have been socialized by a racism woven into the very fabric of American society. Individuals come to understand minority group anger at White society, and they see all minority groups victimized in some way by White racism.

White people in Stage 3 are not sure what their role should be in addressing racism. Feelings of guilt emerge as they contemplate their previously held Stage 2 identity. They harbor negative feelings about whiteness and they are angry at themselves and at other Whites. *Resistance* individuals are likely to attempt to re-educate themselves and other Whites about racism. They will devote time to learning accurate information about other cultures. They may challenge and confront racist institutions through letter writing, boycotts, and demonstrations. At times the Stage 3 individual feels ostracized from other Whites and uncertain about being accepted by minority peers. Stage 3 can be both emotionally draining and stimulating.

Redefinition

Having experienced conflict in Stage 3 between their own values and values deemed appropriate by their racial group, Whites at Stage 4 now begin to search for a new White identity. Whites at the *Redefinition* stage acknowledge the reality and pervasiveness of racism and act to change undesirable situations. This involvement facilitates the development of a more positive White identity. Whites in Redefinition begin to search out aspects of White identity not linked to racism; they learn more about their culture (e.g., Western philosophy, art, and music), and they develop a sense of pride in their group. Importantly, there is a recognition that cultures may vary in values, but no culture or race is superior to another and they all contribute to the enrichment of human life. The Redefinition person is aware of strengths and limitations of White history and culture. She or he has a desire to help other Whites redefine themselves, has empathy for the difficulties Whites have at previous stages, and sees that it is in Whites' self-interest to eradicate racism.

Internalization

Having established a sense of pride in their identity during the previous stage, White people in *Internalization* integrate and incorporate this new racial identity with their overall social identity. A positive White identity is now a healthy part of the individual; it is natural and spontaneous; it requires no conscious thought or effort.

The internalized individual has balanced his or her racial identity with other aspects of identity. Energy is directed toward liberating other Whites from racism and educating themselves about other forms of oppression and their relationship to race (e.g., the interaction of racism and sexism). Internalized Whites voluntarily alienate themselves from some aspects of the social environment and actively engage with other aspects. Table 5.1 outlines the various stages of White racial identity models and roughly displays the relationship of the stages to one another and to general psychosocial development (see discussion of Marcia's work in Chapter Four).

Helms's Model of White Racial Identity Development

Janet Helms (1984) was working independently of Rita Hardiman (1982) when she first conceptualized her White identity model. In recent years,

Table 5.1 Interrelationship of White Racial Identity Models

Models	Stage of Models					
General Identity Model						
Marcia (1980)	Identity Diffusion			Foreclosed Identity	Moratorium	Achieved Identity
White Racial Identity Models						
Hardiman (1982)	No Social Consciousness		Acceptance	Resistance	Redefinition	Internalization
Helms (1990d)	Contact	Disintegration	Reintegration	Pseudo-Independence	Immersion/Emersion	Autonomy
Ponterotto (1988)	Pre-Exposure	Exposure		Zealot/Defensiveness		Integration
Sabnani et al. (1991)	Pre-Exposure/Pre-Contact	Conflict		Pro-Minority/Antiracism	Retreat into White Culture	Redefinition and Integration
Racist Inclinations Associated with Identity Stages	Racially unaware, exhibiting subtle racism	Confused state, exhibiting subtle racism		Racially sensitive, exhibiting subtle racism	Racist Identity	Nonracist Identity

Helms (1990d) has refined and elaborated her theory and has subjected the model to empirical scrutiny (e.g., Carter & Helms, 1990; Helms & Carter, 1990a). In fact, the Helms (1990d) model is the only one that has been operationalized in the form of a published paper-and-pencil assessment (Helms & Carter, 1990b). Helms's (1990d) model consists of six stages organized into two major phases. Phase 1, incorporating the first three stages, is called the *Abandonment of Racism,* and Phase 2, incorporating the last three stages, is termed *Defining a Nonracist White Identity.*

Contact

A White person is in the *Contact* stage as soon as she or he first encounters the idea or actuality that Black people exist. Influenced by family and community, the White person enters the Contact stage with either naive curiosity about Blacks or timidity and trepidation towards Blacks. Usually, Contact stage persons have limited social and occupational interaction with Blacks. Individuals in this stage clearly evaluate Blacks according to White criteria (e.g., White values, see Katz, 1985). Race-focused comments made by individuals in Stage 1 might be: "I don't notice what race a person is"; or "You don't act like a Black person" (Helms, 1990d, p. 57).

Depending on the extent of one's personal interaction with Blacks, Whites can stay in the Contact stage indefinitely. However, as U.S. society becomes increasingly multiracial (see Ponterotto & Casas, 1991) Whites are more likely to have varied contacts with Blacks. If Contact Whites increase their social interactions with Blacks, they may receive the message from the White "in-group" that certain types of interracial contact are inappropriate. At this point it becomes clear to the individual that Blacks and Whites are treated differently in the United States regardless of income level. This realization marks entry into Stage 2.

Disintegration

The *Disintegration* individual acknowledges his or her whiteness and understands the benefits of being White in a racist society. This stage is conflictual in nature: The individual is caught between wanting to be accepted by the norm (White) group, while at the same time experiencing a moral dilemma over treating (or considering) Blacks inferior than Whites. The Disintegration person experiences emotional incongruence because her or his moral belief (e.g., "all people should be treated equally regardless of race") is in direct contrast to in-group expectations. This moral ambivalence results in feelings of guilt, depression, helplessness, and anxiety.

According to Helms (1990d), individuals can respond to and reduce this emotional incongruence and ambivalence in one of three ways: (a) avoid further contact with Blacks, (b) attempt to convince other Whites that Blacks are not inferior, or (c) seek reassurance from Blacks or Whites that racism is not the White person's fault. Helms (1990d, p. 59) notes that

> It seems likely that the person who can remove herself or himself from interracial environments or can remove Blacks from White environments will do so. Given the racial differences in social and economic power, most Whites can choose this option.

When the Disintegration individual conforms to the racist social pressure, she or he has entered the Reintegration stage.

Reintegration Stage

The *Reintegration* person accepts the belief in White racial superiority. The Reintegration identity is essentially a racist identity. Negative conditions associated with Black people are thought to result from Blacks' inferior intellectual, moral, and social qualities. Residual feelings of guilt and anxiety from the Disintegration stage are now transformed into anger and fear towards Black people. There is an effort to protect and preserve White privilege. Whites can remain in the Reintegration stage indefinitely. Often, a personally jarring event is needed to shake the individual from this racist identity. The jarring event might result from an insightful encounter(s) with a White or Black person, or it might be stimulated by changes in the political and social climate (e.g., Civil Rights Movement; the assassination of Dr. Martin Luther King, Jr.). Once the individual has begun to question his or her previous racist identity, Stage 4 is reached.

Pseudo-Independent

The *Pseudo-Independent* stage is the first stage of Phase 2 of the Helms (1990d) model—*Defining a Nonracist White Identity*. At this point individuals begin to acknowledge the responsibilities of Whites for racism. They examine how their own actions or inactions have perpetuated racism and maintained the status quo. Persons at this stage are no longer comfortable with a racist stance and they begin the search for a new White identity. Initially, this search is characterized by an intellectual acceptance and curiosity about Blacks. Helms (1990d) notes that during this search the White person may still behave in ways that unknowingly perpetuate racism. For example, effort is expended in helping Blacks be more like Whites. Furthermore, cultural differences are still interpreted from a White perspective. At this juncture, although the individual has abandoned a negative White identity, she or he has not yet coalesced nor internalized a healthy and positive White identity. In the Pseudo-Independent's quest for a better definition of whiteness, an immersion experience takes place signaling entrance into Stage 5.

Immersion/Emersion

The White person in this stage will often immerse herself or himself in biographies/autobiographies of Whites who have made similar identity journeys. Establishing a positive identity involves re-education, where myths and stereotypes about Blacks and Whites are replaced with accurate information. Whites at this stage attempt to educate and change other Whites. Helms (1990d, p. 62) notes that

> Successful completion of this stage apparently requires emotional catharsis in which the person re-experiences previous emotions that were denied or distorted. . . . Once these negative feelings are expressed, the person may begin to feel euphoria perhaps akin to a religious rebirth.

Autonomy

Autonomy represents the final stage in the White Identity Model. The autonomous person is flexible and open and seeks opportunities to learn about other cultural groups. These individuals also acknowledge and work to eliminate other forms of oppression (e.g., sexism, ageism). A healthy White identity is internalized and acted upon during this stage. Helms emphasizes (as did Cross in his model—see Chapter Four) that although autonomy represents a self-actualization with regard to racial identity, it does not change a person's basic personality structure. For example, an angry and grouchy person at the Contact stage is still an angry and grouchy person at Autonomy, although most likely the person's anger does not center on racial issues.

Ponterotto's White Racial Consciousness Development Model

Ponterotto (1988) presented a four-stage model of racial consciousness development for White counselor trainees. Unlike the Hardiman (1982) and Helms (1990d) models which focus on general White-Black interactions, Ponterotto's model extends to all White-Minority group interactions. Ponterotto (1988) relied on Helms's (1984) first explication of White identity development for theoretical support of his model. Experiential support for the model came from observations of hundreds of White graduate students studying multicultural counseling in the Midwest (Nebraska) and the Northeast (New York). Ponterotto's four-stage model proceeds as follows: Pre-Exposure, Exposure, Zealot-Defensive, and Integration.

Pre-Exposure

In the *Pre-Exposure* stage White graduate students have given little thought to multicultural issues. They are generally naive about both racial issues and their inherited privileges as White people in America. Students in this stage often believe that racism no longer exists, or, that if it does exist, it does so only to a limited degree. Their perceptions of racism are of the old-fashioned type (e.g., Archie Bunker of "All in the Family"); they do not understand or comprehend the notion of subtle or modern racism (refer back to Chapter 2).

Exposure

Students enter the *Exposure* stage when they are first confronted with multicultural issues. In the Ponterotto (1988) model, this occurred when they began their "Multicultural Counseling" course. At this point students are exposed to the realities of continuing racism in the United States. They begin to understand the nature of modern racism and the individual, institutional, and cultural manifestations of racism. Students now acknowledge that Whites and minority-group members are treated differently (regardless of the person's economic status) and that minorities face barriers that White people will never have to deal with. This newfound insight is enlightening to the students, and they initially feel a sense of empowerment over their new and accurate knowledge.

Quickly, however, White students in Exposure begin to realize that they have been lied to throughout their education. They learn that even the counseling profession, which professes to be objective and fair to all, is a tool of institutional and cultural racism because of the profession's centering on White middle class values (cf. Ponterotto & Casas, 1991; Sue & Sue, 1990). Whites in this stage begin to experience anger and guilt—anger over having been deceived for so long and guilt over their naivete in accepting without question myths and stereotypes of minorities fostered by the education system and counseling profession. Students begin to see how they themselves are subtly racist. Their response to these strong emergent feelings signals their entrance into Stage 3.

Zealot-Defensive

Ponterotto (1988) observed that White counseling graduate students often respond to their newfound feelings in one of two ways. Some become very zealous about the multicultural topic. These students dive head first into minority issues, study the topic extensively, and become very pro-minority in philosophy. Ponterotto (1988, p. 152) states that ". . . this pro-minority directed energy enables the student to deal with his or her personal, or White society's collective, guilt in regard to being a White member of society."

Other students respond to their anger and guilt in a very defensive manner. Some students take the criticisms of the "White system" very personally and begin to withdraw from the multicultural topic. Ponterotto (1988) observed that students in this stage would stop participating in class discussions, would now sit in the back of the classroom, and would seldom make eye contact with the professor. These students are quite angry at the professor and see him (in this case) as anti-White.

Integration

Ponterotto (1988) noted that as students were lead to process and express their feelings (guilt, anger, defensiveness), they began to demonstrate a renewed interest and openness to multicultural issues. The intense feelings of Stage 3 attenuate to a large degree and students achieve a more balanced perspective on the topic. At this point the *Integration* stage is achieved. Students now accept the realities of modern racism, they acknowledge their own subtle (and at times not so subtle) racism, and they feel a sense of empowerment about eliminating racism in themselves and in society. Students at this point feel good about themselves as individuals and as members of the White cultural group. They often develop a renewed interest in their racial group (Whites) and their ethnic roots (e.g., Italian, Polish, Irish heritage). There is an appreciation of other cultures and a desire to learn more about various groups. Students also begin to devote energy to other identity commitments such as gender identity, where effort is directed towards understanding and combating sexism.

Integration of White Identity Models

As you noted with the minority identity models presented in Chapter Four, there is a good deal of overlap between the White identity models presented here. Recently, Sabnani, Ponterotto, and Borodovsky (1991) integrated the models of Hardiman (1982), Helms (1984), and Ponterotto (1988) to arrive at an all inclusive model of White racial identity development. The resulting model consists of five stages: Pre-Exposure/Pre-Contact, Conflict, Pro-Minority/Antiracism, Retreat Into White Culture, Redefinition and Integration.

Pre-Exposure/Pre-Contact

All three White identity models posit an initial stage characterized briefly by a lack of awareness of self as a racial being. Hardiman's (1982) Lack of Social Awareness stage and Acceptance stage would fall in this first stage, as would Helms's (1990d) Contact stage, and Ponterotto's (1988) Pre-Exposure stage. White persons in the *Pre-Exposure/Pre-Contact* stage are unaware of social expectations and roles with regard to race and are generally oblivious to cultural/racial issues. They have not yet begun to explore their own racial identity, nor have they given thought to their roles as White people in an oppressive society. At this point there is also an unconscious identification with whiteness and an unquestioned acceptance of stereotypes about minority groups.

Conflict

Stage 2 in the Sabnani et al. (1991) model centers on the construct of conflict over developing race-relations knowledge. At this point there is an expansion of knowledge about racial matters that is facilitated by interactions with members of minority groups or by information gathered elsewhere (e.g., independent reading, a multicultural counseling course). This newly discovered information challenges individuals to acknowledge their whiteness and examine their own cultural values. The central feature of this stage is conflict between wanting to conform to majority norms (i.e., peer pressure from White acquaintances) and wishing to uphold humanistic, nonracist values.

The *Conflict* stage is clearly reflected in all three White identity models. In the transition period from Hardiman's (1982) Acceptance stage to the Resistance stage there is a re-examination of assumptions about White people causing individuals to challenge their accepted ideology about whiteness. Characteristics of Helms's (1990d) Contact and Disintegration stages include the acknowledgment that one is White and feeling caught between White and Black culture and between oppression and humanity. In Ponterotto's (1988) Exposure stage, Whites come face-to-face with minority issues and are challenged to acknowledge the continuing reality of racism and their role in perpetuating the status quo. Key affective components of the Conflict stage are confusion, guilt, anger, and depression.

Pro-Minority/Antiracism

Sabnani et al. (1991) posit that White people often have one of two reactions to the emotional outcomes central to Stage 2. The first response is a strong pro-minority stance. All three models specify a point where Whites begin to resist racism and identify with minority groups. This behavior serves to alleviate some of the strong feelings of guilt and confusion initiated in the previous stage. Hardiman's (1982) Resistance stage involves the rejection of White racist beliefs along with a developing compassion for minority groups. Ponterotto's (1988) Zealot half of his Zealot/Defensive stage is characterized by taking on the minority plight and maintaining a strong pro-minority stance. Characteristics of Helms's (1990d) Disintegration stage include over-identification with and paternalistic attitudes toward Blacks. Whites in Stage 3 experience self-focused anger and guilt over their previous conformity to White socialization as well as anger directed outward toward the White culture in general.

Retreat Into White Culture

Stage 4 is marked by the second of two extremes as a response to the Conflict stage. Whereas some Whites deal with Stage 2 conflict by identifying with minorities, others deal with it by retreating from situations that would stimulate such conflict. This latter response is characterized by a behavioral and attitudinal retreat from interracial contact back into the comfort, security, and familiarity of same-race contacts. White people in the previous Stage 3 are often challenged on their pro-minority views by White peers who sense a racial disloyalty or betrayal. Moreover, these Whites may be confronted by minority peers who question their newfound supportive attitudes. As a result of peer pressure and minority group rejection, some White people feel life would just be easier and less complicated if they retreat into the "White world." Stage 4, therefore, is characterized by an over-identification with whiteness and by a defensiveness about White culture. Helms's (1990d) Reintegration stage describes this anti-Black, pro-White mentality as does Ponterotto's (1988) Defensive half of his Zealot/Defensive stage. Helms notes that this stage is accompanied by fear and anger at Black people.

Redefinition and Integration

All three models posit a point where White people come to redefine what it means to be White in today's society. There is a transition to a more balanced and healthy racial identity. Whites acknowledge their responsibility for maintaining racism while at the same time identifying with a White identity that is nonracist and healthy. They see good and bad in their own group as they do in other groups. Energy is now devoted to nonracial issues and there is an interest in fighting all forms of oppression. Whites at this final stage are flexible and open with regard to culture-learning activities, both from their own racial group and other groups. Ponterotto's (1988) Integration stage would fall in this final stage, as would Hardiman's (1982) Redefinition and Internalization stages, as well as portions of Helms's (1990d) Pseudo-Independence stage and her Immersion-Emersion and Autonomy stages.

Relationship of White Identity Development to Racism

Relative to Black racial identity development, the construct of White identity development is recent in the journal literature and, as a result, has not been subjected to extensive empirical scrutiny. The available research has focused on two related areas: the relationship of White identity to mental health and to levels of racism. The first area covering mental health has received less attention to date and is reviewed first.

Research by Tokar and Swanson (1991) supported the position that Whites in the lower levels of identity development (particularly Helms's

Contact, Disintegration, and Reintegration stages) have achieved lower levels of self-actualization and psychological health than Whites in the final stage (i.e., Helms's Autonomy stage). Focusing on White college women, Taub and McEwen (1992) found lower stages of identity (specifically Disintegration and Reintegration) to be associated with lower scores on a measure of mature interpersonal relationships. Furthermore, this study found Pseudo-Independence attitudes positively correlated to measures of psychosocial autonomy and mature interpersonal relationships, and Autonomy attitudes positively correlated to higher scores on a psychosocial measure of autonomy. In summary these two recent studies support Helms's (1990d) theoretical model.

A growing body of research in recent years has focused on the relationship of White racial identity attitudes to racism. Using Helms' (1984) White identity model as a theoretical base and Helms' and Carter's (1990b) White Racial Identity Attitude Scale as the measurement instrument, Carter (1990) found White racial identity attitudes to be predictive of racism among college students. Specifically, he found that Reintegration and Contact attitudes were related to higher levels of racism. In a replication of the Carter (1990) study, Pope-Davis and Ottavi (in press) also found Reintegration attitudes predictive of racism among college students. Pope-Davis and Ottavi (1992) then replicated their study on a sample of White university faculty members. The authors again found Reintegration attitudes predictive of racism. We should note that there were some gender differences in these three studies and the interested reader should read the respective articles for result and sample specifics.

Claney and Parker (1989) examined the relationship of White racial identity to comfort with Blacks. Using their own White Racial Consciousness Development Scale (a 15-item instrument based on Helms' [1984] model), the authors found a curvilinear relationship between White identity attitudes and college students' reported comfort with Blacks. Specifically, students in the first and last stages reported being more comfortable with Black people, while people in the middle three stages were more uncomfortable around Blacks. These results are consistent with Helms's (1984) model and other White identity models that postulate early stage naivete around racial issues and final stage appreciation and acceptance of racial diversity.

In summary, the results of these studies indicate a relationship among White racial identity attitudes and racism. White persons in Stage 4, Retreat into White Culture, particularly as measured by Helms' model, are more likely to be negatively prejudiced toward Blacks. In the next section of this chapter, we take a closer look a the relevance of these collective findings for race relations in the 1990s.

A Model to Understand Increasing Racial Tensions

White identity theory is a central component in understanding increasing racial tensions in the United States. Recently, Ponterotto (1991) introduced the "Flight or Fight Response Theory of Racial Stress," which explains increasing race-based conflicts in terms of rapid demographic changes interacting with stages of racial identity development.

With regard to demographics, it is now common knowledge that the current White numerical majority will in the next 50 years or so become the numerical minority (Ponterotto & Casas, 1991). These rapid demographic shifts are primarily the result of continued immigration trends from South and Central America and higher fertility rates in some racial and ethnic minority subgroups.

The Flight or Fight Response Theory predicts that as Whites become the numerical minority, they will be more likely to come in contact with racial and ethnic minorities in various contexts. The theory suggests that because of their ethnocentric base, many Whites will feel threatened by the change of demographic status and will either flee from close (nonsuperficial) interracial contact (if possible) or react defensively and in a discriminatory fashion toward minority group members.

In past years when African American children were integrated into predominantly White schools and communities, some White parents moved their children to private schools and their families to all-White neighborhoods. "White flight" to private schools and suburbs was common practice in many urban areas. The frequency or "effectiveness" of the White flight was drastically altered in the 1980s. First, from a sheer numerical perspective, racial and ethnic minority populations were growing rapidly and migrating to more varied geographical regions. Thus White parents could not simply move the household to a "Whiter" community because persons of color were also moving to these communities. Although racial and ethnic minority representation in the middle, upper-middle, and upper socioeconomic strata increased only marginally in the 1980s (see Ponterotto & Casas, 1991 for extensive demographic and economic data), "all White" neighborhoods and schools were becoming more elusive.

Another key factor preventing the White flight tendency was pure economics. Many middle-class White Americans simply could not afford to move the family to the suburbs or enroll their children in predominantly White private schools. The combined effects of extremely rapid demographic changes and White persons' reduced tendency to migrate because of economics resulted in increased intergroup contact in areas of closer proximity.

The Flight or Fight Response Theory of Racial Stress predicts that White Americans who do not migrate away from interethnic contact (the Flight response) have a natural tendency to feel threatened and resort to the Fight response of the theoretical continuum. Although actual physical confrontation is at one end of the theoretical continuum, the Fight response also manifests itself at less intense levels through, for example, heightened prejudicial attitudes and increased ethnic stereotyping.

Figure 5.1 presents the relationship of White identity theory to potential acts of discrimination. The middle column lists Allport's (1979) "Expressions of Prejudice" described in Chapter 3. The far left and far right columns present select stages of the Sabnani et al. (1991) integrated White racial identity development model.

The Flight or Fight Response Theory, with its emphasis on demographic changes, predicts that because of increased interracial contact, more White Americans will be moving from the Pre-Exposure/Pre-Contact stage (where the individual has had minimal interaction with minorities and has not been led to question his or her role as a White individual in a racist society) to the Conflict and Retreat into White Culture stages. As White individuals enter the Conflict stage, they become aware of the realities of racism and the role that individual Whites play in maintaining the status quo. Feelings of guilt, depression, and anxiety emerge. As Figure 5.1 makes clear, some individuals react to these feelings by removing themselves from interracial environments (Avoidance), and some may attempt to remove—or limit—minorities from predominantly White environments (Discrimination).

In the Retreat into White Culture stage the individual has retreated back into the familiarity of an ethnocentric perspective. Residual feelings of fear and anger are now more directed toward persons of color in a number of ways. In a passive expression, individuals may talk more openly and honestly about racial matters to like-minded peers (Antilocution), and may avoid or remove oneself from likely interracial environments (Avoidance). An active expression of Stage 4 attitudes may involve treating minorities as inferior and excluding them from activities (Discrimination), and physically confronting minorities to protect the status quo (Physical Attack stage).

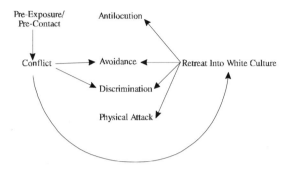

Figure 5.1. Operationalizing the Flight or Fight Response Theory of Racial Stress
NOTE: Some individuals will enter the *Retreat into White Culture* stage directly from the *Conflict* stage, while others will first enter the *Pro-Minority/Anti-Racism stage*. Allport's final stage, *Extermination*, is not included in this model given its absence from current U.S. society. This figure is adapted from Ponterotto (1991) with permission of the American Counseling Association.

The relationships among the Flight or Fight Response Theory, White Racial Identity Theory, and the expressions of prejudice are central to the development of effective prejudice prevention programs. It seems that the development of a positive White identity for Whites (and a minority identity for minority group members) must be a focus of counseling interventions starting at the earliest ages.

Chapter Summary

This chapter has reviewed leading models of White racial identity development. It was emphasized that the development of a healthy nonracist White identity is a long-term developmental task that involves an internal cognitive and affective struggle within the individual. At present, limited research exists examining the relationship between stages of White racial identity and indices of mental health. A more significant body of research is developing which links certain stages to higher levels of prejudice and racism. One promising area for future research is to examine inclusive majority-minority ethnic identity models. The recent work of Smith (1991) is a step in this direction.

This chapter also presented a model termed the "Flight or Fight Response Theory of Racial Stress," which explored the interaction of a rapidly changing demography with racial identity development and potential expressions of prejudice and racism.

A theoretical understanding of racial identity development presented in this and the previous chapter is prerequisite to developing and implementing prejudice-prevention programs. Part III of this book now provides the reader with guidelines for the pragmatic application of prejudice-prevention programs in diverse settings.

PART III

Race Awareness Strategies for the School and Community

Part III of *Preventing Prejudice* focuses on interventions in prejudice prevention. Chapter 6 outlines the ideal conditions for both fostering positive racial identity development and reducing prejudice. This chapter also reviews specific roles counselors can play in their efforts to combat prejudice. Chapters 7 through 9 are devoted to pragmatic interventions for schools, colleges, and the larger community. Enough detail is presented in the exercise descriptions so that counselors and educators can begin implementing these tested activities.

6

Counselor Roles in Prejudice Prevention and Race Relations

Counselors and educators must be at the forefront in teaching and fostering racial/ethnic self-acceptance and interracial tolerance. Counselors, particularly, have a social responsibility to help individuals accept and appreciate themselves and others (Ponterotto, 1991). This chapter examines the diverse roles counselors can play in combating prejudice. The chapter begins with a brief overview of the traditional roles of the counselor. Next we specify four prerequisite emphases for counseling intervention. The chapter concludes with a discussion of five specific roles counselors can play in working on race relations.

Traditional Roles of the Counselor

Three roles have characterized the counseling psychology profession: the remedial, the preventive, and the educative/developmental (Gelso & Fretz, 1992). In remedial work, counselors assist individuals and groups in solving problems that have developed. The remedial role also includes crisis intervention efforts. In preventive work, counselors focus on assisting students and clients to anticipate, circumvent, and possibly forestall problems that may arise. Finally, in educative and developmental work, counselors guide students and clients to seek out and make the best of experiences that will facilitate personal growth.

To a large degree, counselors and educators working in the area of prejudice prevention and race awareness have focused on remedial and crisis intervention efforts. That is, counselors are often called in to deal with racial tensions after they have developed. Schools, colleges, and communities have often relied upon educators and counselors to diffuse racial animosities.

It is our view that counselors and educators need to direct more effort to the preventive and educative/developmental aspects of prejudice prevention. A main emphasis of this book is that developing a healthy respect for other cultures is a long-term developmental process. This process begins with developing a healthy sense of one's own racial/ethnic identity. Through preventive and psychoeducational interventions, counselors and educators can contribute greatly to enhancing racial/ethnic identity development and reducing prejudice.

Counselor Skills and Prejudice Prevention Work

Counselors are ideally trained to work in the area of race awareness and prejudice prevention. Counseling professionals are highly skilled in interpersonal communication, crisis intervention and conflict resolution (e.g., Lane & McWhirter, 1992; McFarland, 1992), social influence, behavior and attitude change, and human development. (Educators and administrators as well have important skills that can be extended to prejudice prevention work.) This cadre of theoretical bases and concomitant skills equip counselors with important tools to study, prevent, and combat prejudice.

In their day-to-day work in schools, colleges, and communities, counselors (and educators) need to emphasize five areas that are central to effective prejudice-prevention programming: (a) facilitating healthy ethnic identity development in students and clients of all ages, (b) fostering critical thinking skills, (c) promoting multicultural and nonsexist education, (d) facilitating interracial contact, and (e) focusing on transforming negative racial attitudes.

Facilitating Healthy Ethnic Identity Development

As we learned in Chapters 4 and 5, some research evidence suggests that people of all races who have reached higher stages of racial/ethnic identity development are more likely to have better mental health and to possess lower levels of prejudice and racism. The education and mental health systems, however, have neglected the area of racial identity development, focusing instead on occupational, religious, and gender-role identity. We believe racial/ethnic identity development needs to be nourished and encouraged on the same level as the more traditional foci of human development (see also Phinney & Rotheram, 1987a).

To promote healthy racial/ethnic identity development in their students and clients, educators and counselors must first understand racial/ethnic identity development theory. Second, they must assess their own levels of racial/ethnic identity development and then take proactive steps to further develop their racial identity. Finally, they must be trained in facilitating racial/ethnic identity development in others. The five emphases for prejudice-prevention work specified in this section are a starting point for counselors and educators working in the area. Furthermore, strategies to reduce prejudice and enhance racial/ethnic identity development form the foundation of the next three chapters. Another good source is Helms (in press) who recently outlined strategies for enhancing racial identity development in Black and White school children.

Fostering Critical Thinking Skills

Cognitively sophisticated children are less likely to become prejudiced adolescents and adults than are children who "think" simply and unquestioningly (Gabelko, 1988). Walsh (1988) has provided a valuable contribution to our topic through her integration of work on critical thinking (D'Angelo, 1971) with prejudice prevention. She presents 10 factors related to the climate for and the development of critical thinking (or cognitive sophistication; Gabelko, 1988) in children. Below we paraphrase and expand upon Walsh's (1988) ten points.

Climate of respect and trust. For students to challenge their own thinking and that of others, teachers and counselors must create an atmosphere of trust and support in the classroom or group setting. Children (and adults) are not likely to share personal thoughts and feelings if they fear being ridiculed. We suggest teachers and counselors set ground rules (much the way counselors do in group counseling situations) for the discussion of prejudice and other topics. Such ground rules would include requiring students to respect others' opinions, allowing students to finish their statements before being challenged, and so forth.

Community of inquiry. Counselors and educators can help students learn to ask the right questions instead of focusing solely on getting the "right" answers. Furthermore, not all questions have one right answer; some may have multiple correct responses.

Allow students to be heard. Students need to feel that their thoughts, opinions, and feelings matter. They need to be heard and listened to, just as the counselor or educator expects to be listened to. Students should be led to discuss and grapple with ideas and problems.

Self-esteem and success. Evidence points to a strong correlation between high self-esteem and lower levels of prejudice (Byrnes, 1988; Pate, 1988; Walsh, 1988). Educators and counselors need to foster self-esteem development in children, adolescents, and adults. Building a healthy sense of racial identity contributes to this process, as does ensuring that students reach success levels in the classroom.

Analyze thinking. Walsh (1988, p. 18) notes that "getting students to think about their thinking is extremely important." Students can be led to analyze their thought process in arriving at decisions.

Intellectual curiosity and being systematic. It is important that students be methodical when considering a problem. Walsh (1988) suggests that after identifying a topic, students should brainstorm and then plan carefully the questions of greatest importance to the topic.

Objectivity and respect for diverse viewpoints. It is common nature to believe your position or viewpoint is the "best" or only "right" one. It is easy to see how this rigidity could facilitate stereotypical thinking and lower levels of racial/ethnic identity development. Using debates where students take both sides of an issue could facilitate cognitive flexibility. Also, as mentioned earlier, setting ground rules for discussion (e.g., allowing assertive expression but not aggression or name calling, etc.) serves as an important strategy to promote critical thinking.

Flexibility and open-mindedness. A challenge for educators and counselors is to teach our students and counselors to be open-minded and flexible. Do our students make judgments without bias and prejudice? Can they consider a variety of beliefs and views as equally legitimate, although different? Are they willing to change their beliefs or methods of inquiry to expand their perceptions? These questions pose important challenges to professionals given that it is human nature to cherish one's beliefs and opinions. Individuals with lower self-esteem may be particularly rigid, as the thought of being "wrong" can be ego-threatening. Once again we see the need to promote healthy self-esteem development in children and adolescents.

Decisiveness. Although it is important to consider alternate positions on an issue, it is equally important to reach and defend a conclusion when the evidence warrants. For example, we, the authors of *Preventing Prejudice,* have reached the conclusion that prejudice and racism continue to be pervasive problems in the United States and abroad. Yes, we were flexible and did consider competing interpretations of recent events. For example, we explored the theory that prejudice is not a major problem but that it is perceived so simply because the media have been more insistent on its coverage. We reviewed the research, we interviewed many people, and we ran countless focus and discussion groups. For us, the evidence is conclusive that racism is a major world-wide problem. An important component of critical thinking is to be able to take a stand and present a position that is supported by evidence.

Intellectual honesty. It is easy to be swayed by emotional appeals for support of a given topic. Students can be taught to distinguish between appeals to reason and appeals to emotion. By analyzing reports (e.g., newspaper accounts, biographies, history) in terms of the language used (e.g., quality of reasoning, extent of rhetoric and emotionally laden language), adolescents and adults can become effective at assessing the credibility of sources.

Promoting Multicultural and Nonsexist Education

Multicultural and nonsexist (see McCormick, 1990) education from the preschool years to the college years is a prerequisite to the establishment of a culturally tolerant and accepting society. A culturally pluralistic education is certainly enhanced and facilitated through the use of the critical thinking skills discussed above.

Traditional models of education are ethnocentric in that they espouse White middle class values (e.g., individualism, competition, time linearity, nuclear family preference, and the Christian perspective; see Ponterotto & Casas, 1991 for an extensive discussion) as the norm, which all cultures are expected to emulate. Culturally diverse value systems (e.g., group or tribe priority over individual achievement, cooperation instead of competition, a circular instead of linear time frame, and an extended family perspective versus a nuclear family emphasis) are not given equivalent value in traditional models of education and mental health. Multicultural education "refers to materials and programs that foster understanding and appreciation of ethnic diversity and promote positive interethnic relations" (Phinney & Rotheram, 1987b, p. 277). Cultural pluralism in education is characterized by an atmosphere in which differences are appreciated and shared, and in which students from various racial/ethnic backgrounds feel equally comfortable as learners in school.

There is considerable debate whether multicultural education should address cross-cultural similarities *or* differences (see review in Phinney & Rotheram, 1987b). A balanced focus on similarities *and* differences is now recommended in general education (Ponterotto et al., 1990) and in counselor education (Ponterotto & Benesch, 1988; Ponterotto & Casas, 1991). Understanding similarities demonstrates that humans are more alike than different, thus creating a shared collaborative perspective. It is also important to focus on cultural differences, for such differences will be noted anyway, and through proper education differences can be interpreted as equally valid, although different. If differences across cultures are not acknowledged and discussed, they will be interpreted as "less than," fostering a culturally deficient or culturally disadvantaged depiction of minority education and minority mental health.

Facilitating Interracial Contact

An important component of racial identity development and multicultural appreciation is having interpersonal contact with people of diverse cultures. However, it is important to emphasize what kind of contacts are most helpful. Integrated schooling and other interethnic contact forms do not in and of themselves promote harmonious relationships. According to the well-researched Contact Hypothesis (see Brewer & Miller, 1984; Phinney & Rotheram, 1987b), a number of conditions must be satisfied if interethnic contact is to promote positive relationships. First, there must be equal status between individuals in the given context. In contrast, contact in a hierarchical system, or between individuals who perceive one another as a threat, or between people who equally *lack* status (poor Whites and poor Blacks), lead to increased prejudice (Allport, 1979). Second, the contact must be substantial enough (not casual or superficial) to allow the interethnic dyad to disconfirm stereotypes about the respective groups.

Third, the contact should revolve around necessary interdependence to achieve group goals. Fourth, the situation or context must include social norms that favor the respective groups equally.

Educators and counselors can incorporate cooperative learning activities to foster interethnic appreciation. When individuals share common tasks, problems, goals, and rewards with culturally diverse peers, positive interethnic feelings emerge (Byrnes, 1988; Pate, 1988).

Focusing on Transforming Negative Racial Attitudes

To combat the roots of prejudice effectively, multicultural awareness programs must address individuals' attitudes. Naturally, critical thinking skills facilitate this process. In our earlier definition of prejudice (refer back to Chapter One), we noted both a belief and attitude component. Allport (1979) stresses that individual beliefs (e.g., "All Asian Americans are wealthy") can be altered in the face of factual evidence, but that the underlying attitude at the root of the erroneous belief is more resistant to change. An individual with prejudicial attitudes can quickly present another erroneous belief for each one that is refuted by factual evidence. Allport (1979, pp. 13-14) presents a cogent example of this tendency in the following anti-Semitic vignette:

Mr. X: The trouble with the Jews is that they only take care of their own group.

Mr. Y: But the record of the Community Chest campaign shows that they give more generously, in proportion to their numbers, to the general charities of the community, than do non-Jews.

Mr. X: That shows they are always trying to buy favor and intrude into Christian affairs. They think of nothing but money; that is why there are so many Jewish bankers.

Mr. Y: But a recent study shows that the percentage of Jews in the banking business is negligible, far smaller than the percentage of non-Jews.

Mr. X: That's just it; they don't go in for respectable business; they are only in the movie business or run nightclubs.

This example highlights how forcefully an underlying attitude may be resistant to change, even in the face of factual evidence. In designing prejudice prevention programs, counselors must work on modifying these stubborn, ingrained attitudes. Simply attempting to change a racial belief by presenting students and clients with accurate factual knowledge about the specific group will do little good. Counselors need to penetrate the attitudinal wall underlying the racial belief; to do so often necessitates experiential and affective interventions. Samples of these interventions constitute the bulk of the next three chapters. First, however, it is important to specify various roles counselors can play in prejudice-prevention work.

Counselor Roles in Prejudice Prevention

Counselors can be more involved in multicultural-awareness training at all developmental levels. The specific roles they can play involve parent training, faculty and administrative consultation, group counseling and support, individual and family counseling, and the counselor as activist. Although some of these roles are more relevant to a professional counselor's training (i.e., individual, family, and group counseling), other roles fall clearly within the training and work environments of educators and administrators. Ideally, professionals from these diverse disciplines would work in an interdisciplinary fashion.

Parent Training

Katz (1987) states that: "Although parents generally have been blamed for negative intergroup attitudes in their children, there has been remarkably little attempt to provide parents with methods of raising children with positive attitudes toward themselves and others" (p. 99).

As noted earlier, school- and campus-based interventions will not go very far if students leave school to enter ethnocentric households and communities. Young children, particularly, need the approval of their parents, and if "White superiority" is the family norm, then young children will nourish this norm. Counselors can consider speaking to parent groups, as most schools already have formal and informal mechanisms for school-parent dialogue. Again, parents must be instilled with the attitude that cultural diversity in and of itself is rewarding, and that the students are academically and socially enriched by diversity. Counselors can collaborate with teachers and administrators in the development of culturally diverse and multilingual pamphlets focusing on cultural pluralism. The innovative work of Casas and Furlong (in press) with bilingual storybooks for children and their parents provides a model with great impact.

Parent training in multicultural appreciation should not be limited to preschool through high school. Many colleges and universities have parent orientation weekends, and cultural similarity and diversity issues should be a component of such programs.

Faculty and Administration Consultants

Many faculty and administrators were not trained in a culturally plural-istic atmosphere, and although well-intentioned, they are most likely cultur-ally encapsulated (Wrenn, 1985) and ethnocentric (Ponterotto & Casas, 1991). Unfortunately, many counselors, as well, are ill-equipped to work in a culturally diverse environment (Ponterotto & Casas, 1987). Nonethe-less, given the counseling profession's recent emphasis on multicultural training reflected in program accreditation criteria and in new certification and licensure plans, counselors are becoming more aware of and skilled in multicultural mental health. Counselors can be involved in continuing education projects for faculty and staff, and they can serve as individual consultants to faculty seeking culturally relevant course curriculum ma-terials, or requesting advice on, for example, the role of culture on cognitive and learning styles or expected teacher-student relationship styles.

Group Counseling and Support

Counselors are trained group facilitators, and, in some cases, group formats may be an ideal way to discuss and deal with prejudice. Mixed racial groups provide an ideal route to culture sharing, to hearing firsthand the effects of prejudice and discrimination on individual group members, and to establishing empathic understanding.

In terms of conflict resolution and crisis intervention, counselors may first work with same-race groups to allow for free and uninhibited cathar-tic expression. Allport (1979) noted that "In part, catharsis may be effective because one's irrational outburst shocks one's own conscience" (p. 498). At that point, interracial groups can be run. Whether to run same-race or interracial support or process groups will vary by the specific situation, the ages of the clients, and the emotional tension present in the school. Counselors should consult with campus and community minority leaders and one another before deciding on the specific group approach.

Individual and Family Counseling

If prejudice is deeply embedded in one's personality, counseling and therapy may be required to modify attitudes. Students involved in more active expressions of prejudice, for example *discrimination* and *physical attacks* (refer back to Chapter 3), may be required to see a counselor for a specified period of time. Naturally, the counselor can expect either re-sistance or faked acquiescence in the initial stages of counseling;

nonetheless, a skilled counselor could assist such a client. Again, group counseling may be an option for students violating school principles and civil rights mandates. Given the growing body of conceptual and empirical knowledge on White racial identity development and minority identity development models, it appears that the development of a healthy and positive ethnic identity should be a focus of individual and group counseling, as well as general multicultural education (Atkinson et al., 1989; Helms, 1984, 1990a; Parham, 1989; Ponterotto, 1988; Ponterotto & Casas, 1991; Ruiz, 1990; Sabnani, Ponterotto, & Borodovsky, 1991; White & Parham, 1990).

An option that is not discussed in the literature is family counseling focusing on prejudice awareness and prevention. If we can assume that the family, particularly parents and older siblings, play a pivotal role "teaching" prejudice to children, then family counseling may provide effective avenues for family attitude change.

The Counselor as Activist

In addition to working with individuals, families, and small groups, counselors can impact society on a larger scale. Through their own professional activism, counselors, along with their parent organization, the American Counseling Association (ACA) and related professional organizations, can influence the media and lobby the federal government for supportive legislation. Below we focus on the areas of television and federal legislation.

A powerful socializing factor confronting children and parents is television. With all the technical, scholarly, and pragmatic resources available to the American Counseling Association (ACA), the organization might consider producing television programs that facilitate cultural harmony for both children and adults. Naturally, such a powerful and far-reaching media strategy could be used to promote other social issues as well. Most children and adults do not work with counselors in any significant capacity, and if we are to reach a majority of the population, we must access common communication channels.

In addition to working through the media, ACA can be more involved in multicultural education and prejudice-prevention programs by way of accreditation, funding, and corporate collaborative efforts. Both Brown (1990) and Casas (1990) recently presented interesting and thought-provoking discussions on this topic.

A final point dealing with prejudice prevention concerns federal legislation and Presidential Executive Orders. Some proponents of affirmative action believe that the Reagan/Bush years, which witnessed a more conservative "color-blind" approach to affirmative action, have stalled—if not reversed—the civil rights gains of the 1960s and 1970s (see extensive discussions in Ponterotto et al., 1990). The affirmative action programs struck down by the Supreme Court in the last decade have provided fuel to already held prejudicial, anti-affirmative-action attitudes held by many Americans. The American Counseling Association can be more involved in lobbying government for support of civil rights and affirmative action for racial/ethnic minorities and women, as well as for other oppressed groups (see Atkinson & Hackett, 1988). Allport (1979) provides convincing evidence that Presidential Executive Orders and Supreme Court decisions, if enforced, serve as sharp tools in the battle against discrimination. It appears that although legislation is intended to control outward expressions of intolerance, such laws may, over time, affect inner attitudes and feelings.

Chapter Summary

This chapter has emphasized the need for increased counselor and educator involvement in the area of racial/ethnic identity development and race relations. It is clear that for prejudice-prevention efforts to succeed they must be multifaceted and ongoing. Multicultural sensitivity training must begin with parents and follow children throughout their development. It is important to realize that *teaching about* prejudice is not sufficient. Counseling professionals need to foster racial identity development, critical thinking skills, and multicultural education in their efforts to promote interracial harmony.

This chapter has provided a general overview of what roles counselors and educators can play to facilitate racial harmony. Chapter 7 now takes a closer look at specific exercises counselors can utilize to help promote multicultural understanding in school children.

7

Race Relations in the Schools

Prejudice prevention in the schools is especially important because it is at this stage of life that adolescents learn to depend on their cognitive capabilities and are more comfortable with abstract reasoning. It is also at this stage that the psychosocial tasks such as peer affiliation become more important.

Pedersen (in press) combines the intervention agenda with a training and educational model. School students may be more attracted to the educational approach of "learning" about prejudice and prejudice prevention than to the medical model of "treatment." It is also important to focus on training or prejudice prevention that includes the faculty and staff, as well as students, so that the whole system can be changed, rather than attempting to change the school student in isolation from the rest of the school-community culture.

By 1995 three out of every five U.S. school students will belong to a minority culture. And yet, these numbers do not really capture the subjective experience of racism for either Whites or Non-Whites. The numbers are shallow representations of family members and their personal experiences for many of our students. However, the numbers are necessary, and it is often through those abstract numbers that most Whites first become conscious of the reality of racism.

> This reliance on the quantification of racism not only denies the experiences
> of individuals, it also creates a public perception that racism is only a residual
> effect of other social indices, and does not constitute a real and present issue
> in life in the United States (Hidalgo, McDowell & Siddle, 1990, p. 1).

In previous chapters we have discussed the process of ethnic, racial, and cultural identity and the role of that identity in prejudice prevention. We know (Sherif & Sherif, 1953) that social influence is particularly strong when the facts are ambiguous and that this social influence is seen through both the formation of "in-groups" and "intergroup" friction or conflict. Tajfel (1970) speaks of social identity and social differentiation growing out of a "We" versus a "They" orientation as a necessary but not sufficient condition for reducing intergroup conflict. We also know from Festinger (1954) that we develop our self-concept through social comparison with others. Prejudice, war, aggression, and discrimination persist as natural phenomena in society. Only when we come to understand this process more adequately can we hope to escape the potential destructive force that prejudice presents.

Many states (e.g., California, Pennsylvania, North Carolina, and Minnesota) have required multicultural training for the recertification of school personnel for some time. Minnesota was one of the first states to require (through regulation EDU 521 in 1973) that all teachers complete a training program in human relations training to develop intercultural skills. Teachers were trained to: (a) understand the contributions and life styles of the various racial, cultural and economic groups in our society; (b) recognize and deal with dehumanizing biases, discrimination and prejudices; (c) create learning environments that contribute to the self-esteem of all persons and to positive interpersonal relations; (d) respect human diversity and personal rights (Filla & Clark, 1973).

Other school systems have also implemented programs to help teachers and students to work with students from minority cultures, from homes where English is not spoken, with handicapping conditions, or who are gifted or talented students. On May 19, 1989, the State Education Department of the State University of New York submitted a plan to the Board of Regents for increasing students' knowledge and understanding of diverse peoples. This plan will emphasize a greater understanding at the K-12 levels of American history and culture, the history and culture of the diverse groups that constitute American society today, and the history and culture of other peoples throughout the world (Sobol, 1990). Canadian schools are also working on programs to emphasize career development resources and strategies for working with youth of various racial, ethnic and cultural backgrounds (James, 1990). Although there is no consensus about an appropriate response to prejudice in schools there is a widespread recognition of prejudice as a serious problem.

When we teach prejudice prevention we are really teaching people about their own identity in a context of many others whose identities are different. The students need to be aware of their own developing identity both as they see it and as others around them see it. One way to teach the importance of real and perceived identity is with a *label* exercise.

Exercise #1:   The Label Game

Objective:

To generalize from feedback by others to discover the labeled identity that others perceive you to have.

Procedure:

1. Prepare a variety of *positive* labels of adjectives (such as Friendly, Helpful, Sexy, Generous, Loving, and so on) on sticky address labels with enough labels for all students.

2. Attach one label to the forehead of each student as the student comes into the room. If it would be a cultural taboo to attach the label to the student's forehead then attach it to the student's back so that the student cannot read it.

3. Allow the students to mingle and interact on a topic of interest to them or set up a "cocktail party" scene with no structure.

4. Students will be instructed to treat every other individual as though the label that individual is wearing were actually true, thereby saying and doing the things you would say or do to or with that kind of person. It might be useful to divide larger groups into smaller clusters of six or eight students who interact with one another.

5. No student is allowed to ask another student to tell what the label says, and students are discouraged from looking at their own reflections to read their label.

6. After 10 minutes of interacting students are instructed to *first* guess what the label says and *then* remove the label to see if they were accurate.

Debriefing:

In the discussion following this exercise students are encouraged to disclose how they decoded feedback from others to discover their labels.

Students are also encouraged to discuss how they felt about being labeled and treated as though the label were accurate. The concepts of stereotyping, prejudice, and communication barriers can be introduced using examples from the exercise.

Learning Principle:

We all wear labels that are perceived by others around us who treat us as though the labels were true. By increasing awareness, we can become more aware of the labels that others perceive about each of us.

If it is not possible to get everyone to agree with one another and work together as a group, the next best outcome is to help people see the great diversity around them. If you cannot get the students to see how we are all the same—at least on some things—the next best thing is to show them how we are all different. The *least* favorable and the *most* destructive outcome is when the group divides itself into a two-sided polarity of "Us" and "Them," where each side is against the other. This polarization is like a "war" setting and is to be avoided. The notion of diversity must be taught in such a way that the students can see that there are real differences, that being different is not always bad, and that differences are always important to a person's identity. It is particularly hard to teach diversity to younger children. Exercise #2 suggests one way that this construct can be taught.

Exercise #2:   Patterns of Differences

Objective:

We belong to many different groups that function in ways similar to cultures and define our multicultural identity. This exercise was used to teach primary schoolchildren the many groups to which they belong, including nationality and ethnicity, which define them as individuals.

Procedure:

1. Assemble a group of elementary school students in a large room in which all furniture, tables, chairs, and so on, are moved to the side or the corner of the room. (The exercise may create noise, so it should be scheduled at a time not disruptive to other classes.)
2. The exercise may begin with a story or talk about prejudice, discrimination, or problems that persons who are "different" may have experienced.

3. The students are assembled into a cluster in the center of the room to await instructions.
4. The teacher or leader will have drawn up a list ahead of time of contrasting characteristics that are likely to divide the group. These may include, for example, such neutral characteristics as black shoes and brown shoes, those wearing red and those not wearing red, those with a penny in their pocket and those without a penny in their pocket.
5. The teacher reads out the instructions, saying: "All those with (name the characteristic) go to this side of the room and all those without (name the characteristic) go to the other side of the room." In this way two "teams" will be formed, one team with the named characteristic and one team with a contrasting characteristic. The team whose members identify their similarity first and get all the team members together on their side of the room first "wins" that set.
6. Then the total group reassembles in the middle of the room, and a second set begins with the teacher reading off a new set of contrasting characteristics that will divide the group differently.
7. After the students have become more familiar with the exercise the teacher might want to move toward more personal characteristics such as hair color, height, gender, nationality, and ethnicity.

Debriefing:

After about 20 minutes the teacher could begin a group discussion on how racial differences are just one of the very significant components of our individuality that define us but should not be seen in isolation. The discussion might include the role of competition—winning and losing—in the exercise where the students were on different teams for each set and not rigidly locked into the same group all the time. The students might be encouraged to talk about how they felt about being different from some students and similar to others.

Learning Principle:

You will always be similar to some people and different from others but, depending on the situation, the group to which you belong might change.

Sometimes it is hard for younger students to talk about their culture because that discussion would be too abstract. Although differences do matter—in the sense that each set has a winner and a loser—they don't always have to set the same groups against one another. No matter how different the person or group is, there will be similarities. No matter how similar the person or group is, there will be differences. Exercise #3 is an attempt to look at the symbols of our culture.

Exercise #3:   Symbols of Our Culture

Objective:

Sometimes we become so dependent on abstract verbal jargon about prejudice and racial identity that we lose touch with the less cognitive and more emotional symbols of our cultures. By asking persons to draw the symbols of their culture that may include anything *but* words, participants are encouraged to explore the less articulate parts of their racial identity.

Procedure:

1. Students are assembled in a room with sufficient table space so that each one can spread out a large sheet of paper. Large sheets of poster paper work well if there is sufficient space to spread them out.
2. Students are provided with different colored crayons or felt marking pens with which to draw.
3. Students are instructed to draw symbols, a picture-story, lines, designs, or scribbles on the paper that symbolize their own personal ethnic, racial, or cultural identity.
4. Students are instructed *not* to draw or write "words" on the paper.
5. Students are allowed to draw whatever they want to (except words) for about ten to twenty minutes.
6. After drawing the symbols of their culture, students are assembled into small groups of about five persons.
7. Each student is asked to explain his or her drawing and how those drawings symbolize significant parts of the student's ethnic, racial, or cultural identity.
8. After each group of five students has had about a half-hour for members to present and explain the symbols of their culture, the total group of participants is assembled for a discussion.

Debriefing:

The teacher may want the students to discuss which symbols appeared most often and least often in the drawings, which symbols were the strongest and most powerful, which symbols indicated a positive experience, and which symbols indicated a negative experience. The teacher might want to ask whether any of the symbols were "hard to explain" in words, pointing out how words are not always adequate to express what we feel about our ethnic, racial and cultural identity. Allowing the drawings to hang in the room might be useful to continue the discussion of these symbols among the students.

Learning Principle:

Symbols of our ethnic, racial, and cultural identity may be difficult to discuss in words but nonetheless be very important to the individual.

Students in secondary schools regularly report instances of "bullying" where one student is isolated from the group and punished for being different. The difference may be in how the student looks, in clothes, in level of achievement, or some other distinguishing feature. In some countries, such as Japan, bullying is taking so seriously among adolescents that it can lead to a student committing suicide. It is important for students to accept themselves, even if they are not "typical" for their reference group. Exercise #4 looks at the ways the student is different as well as the positive and negative consequence of that difference.

Exercise #4:   Being Normal and Being Abnormal

Objective:

We are used to thinking of the construct "normal" both as the way *most* people are and/or the way most people *should* become. We therefore help persons "adapt" to this notion of normal so that they can become "well adjusted." This exercise looks at both the positive and the negative consequences of a student being "different" from the different reference groups to which he or she belongs.

Procedure:

1. Copies of a work sheet are distributed among secondary school students indicating twelve or more reference groups.
2. With each reference group, the work sheet indicates that there are positive and negative consequences.
3. Students are instructed to complete the work sheet indicating how they are "different" from other typical members of that group, as the student defines "typical."

4. Students are then instructed to indicate both the positive and the negative consequences of being different.

5. The work sheet will include the following categories:

Ethnicity	Place of residence
positive	positive
negative	negative
Nationality	Social status
positive	positive
negative	negative
Religion	Economic status
positive	positive
negative	negative
Language	Educational status
positive	positive
negative	negative
Age	Formal affiliation
positive	positive
negative	negative
Gender	Informal affiliation
positive	positive
negative	negative

Debriefing:

Some of the students will find some reference group categories easier to discuss than others. In other cases students may be able to discover only positive or only negative consequences to being different. By sharing both the positive and the negative side of being different, the complex within-group differences of ethnic, racial, and cultural identity groups becomes more clearly defined, both in terms of positive and negative consequences.

Learning Principle:

Being different will have both positive and negative consequences for a person's ethnic, racial, or cultural identity.

A first step in prejudice prevention is becoming aware of one's own cultural biases. We often presume that while others may have cultural bias, we are relatively free of bias in our own lives. This "self-reference criterion" leads us toward what Wrenn (1985) called "cultural encapsulation." In Exercise #5, students are asked to identify specific adjectives describing stereotypes that might be held regarding a particular ethnic, racial, or cultural group.

Exercise #5:   Stereotypes

Objective:

Sometimes, by focusing on stereotypes directly and explicitly, it is possible to increase our control over the ways that stereotypes shape our lives. This exercise provides the opportunity for persons to describe "typical" or "frequently expressed" stereotypes about different groups, even though the participant does not believe that stereotype. Students from different ethnic, racial, and cultural groups will probably identify different patterns of stereotypes. By testing these stereotypes against persons actually from the different groups, it should be possible to demonstrate the dangers of stereotyping.

Procedure:

1. Assemble a group of students willing to look at stereotypes regarding different ethnic, racial, and cultural groups. Because the topic is sensitive, it would be useful to keep the groups small, from 5 to 10 persons, for instance. It would also be useful to include different ethnic, racial, and cultural group members among the participants.
2. Each participant will be asked to complete a checklist indicating different ethnic, racial, and cultural groups at the top of the page and a list of adjectives along one side of the page.

Adjectives	Groups				
	A	B	C	D	E
not at all aggressive					
conceited about appearance					
very ambitious					
almost always acts as a leader					
very independent					
does not hide emotions					
very active					
very logical					

Adjectives	Groups				
	A	B	C	D	E
not at all competitive					
feelings easily hurt					
not at all emotional					
very strong need for security					
easily influenced					
very objective					
very self-confident					
easy going					
has difficulty making decisions					
dependent					
likes math and science					
very passive					
very direct					
knows the ways of the world					
excitable in a minor crisis					
very adventurous					
very submissive					
hard-working and industrious					
not comfortable with aggression					

Debriefing:

Students may work in small groups to compare patterns of similarity and difference as they identify stereotypes typically held regarding one or another ethnic, racial, or cultural group. Because stereotypes tend to be volatile and emotion-laden, it is not necessary for individual participants to indicate whether or not they themselves agree with the stereotypes— although their acceptance or rejection of the stereotype may well come out in the discussion. It would be useful to test these stereotypes against actual persons who are members of the ethnic, racial, cultural groups being mentioned. It might also be useful to search through magazines or publications to find pictures or word descriptions that do or do not support the stereotypes.

Learning principle:

Stereotypes are most powerful when they are unexamined and untested against the reality of the ethnic, racial, or cultural groups being represented. Individual differences are what you were born with. Ethnic, racial, and cultural differences are the result of everything that has happened to you since then. It is especially crucial to prevent prejudice in the adolescent years when identity is being shaped and where ethnic, racial, and cultural differences have such a profound impact. In Exercise #6, we look at the unfolding process by which a person's ethnic, racial, and cultural identity is developed.

Exercise #6:   Personal Culture History

Objective:

History is often underemphasized both as it relates to individuals and groups of individuals in the U.S. national culture. Many cultures believe that the extent to which a person knows his or her own history determines the person's level of civilization. This exercise focuses on significant and influential events in a person's own historical development that will help that person see the patterns of ethnic, racial, and cultural identity development as it occurred. By being more aware of our own personal cultural history and by comparing our histories with others we can become more aware of both our similarities and our differences.

Procedure:

1. Assemble a small group of about five students willing to discuss their own personal cultural history.
2. Ideally, this group will be multicultural, that is, from different ethnic, racial, and cultural groups.
3. Each student is given a list of seven questions and asked to answer each question briefly on paper.
4. When all the students have examined each question, the facilitator will ask each person in turn to respond to the first question and discuss her or his answer.
5. Each of the seven questions will be discussed in turn, going on to the next question when every student has had an opportunity to present his or her answer to the previous question. The questions are as follows:
   a. Describe the earliest memory you have of an experience with a person (people) of a cultural or ethnic group different from your own.

b. Who or what has had the most influence in the formation of your attitudes and opinions about people of different cultural groups and in what ways?

c. What influences in your experiences have led to the development of positive feelings about your own cultural heritage and background?

d. What influences in your experiences have led to the development of negative feelings, if any, about your own cultural heritage or background?

e. What changes, if any, would you like to make in your own attitudes or experiences in relation to people of other ethnic or cultural groups?

f. Describe an experience in your own life in which you feel you were discriminated against for any reason, not necessarily because of your culture.

g. How do you feel _____ (fill in the blank with the name of an ethnic, racial, or cultural group) should deal with issues of cultural diversity in American life?

Debriefing:

The debriefing of students will take place during the exercise as each of the seven questions is discussed in turn by each of the participants. The facilitator will want to point out the process by which ethnic, racial, and cultural identity is developed and how prejudice prevention can be implemented.

Learning Principle:

Ethnic, racial, and cultural identity develops as a result of good and bad experiences in one's life that frequently involve prejudice.

Chapter Summary

We have examined six different exercises designed to increase awareness of ethnic, racial, and cultural identity. These exercises are designed to help the student become more aware of how prejudice happens. Prejudice happens when the normal process of comparing yourself to others gets out of control.

Prejudice happens when the expectation you have in your own mind of someone else becomes more important than the real, live individual standing in front of you. Prejudice happens when you force other people to fit your own expectations for them. Prejudice happens when you've lost control of your own life and let others make your decisions for you.

8

Race Relations on the College Campus

The previous chapter was focused on schoolchildren in school who were working with identity issues, affiliation needs and other developmental psychosocial tasks. The emphasis in the chapter was on building a systematic awareness of racial identity and the basic underlying assumptions that have been taught to school-aged youth by their cultures. This chapter will focus primarily on the second stage of multicultural development by emphasizing the importance of knowledge or, perhaps better yet, "comprehension" of the facts and information about our ethnic and racial cultural identities and how they work.

The incidence of ethnoviolence on college campuses has been increasing rapidly across the country. D'Souza's (1991) recent attack on affirmative action programs at universities as having resulted in "illiberal education" demonstrates the increased polarization of forces at colleges and universities. On one hand, the increased visibility of minorities on campus and increased awareness of institutional racism on campus has led to multicultural curriculum requirements, training programs, and the development of new courses focused directly on minority concerns. In some (and perhaps many) cases, these attempts to implement affirmative action to right a wrong and to move the curriculum toward accuracy, have been less than successful. This has particularly been true when the affirmative action has been more a cosmetic adjustment to meet the appearance of equity without allowing any real change to occur, in reluctant response to special interest pressure groups.

On the other hand, there is a backlash by persons who believe that affirmative action is destroying the foundations of university education. D'Souza (1991) has become a spokesperson for the critics of affirmative action. In the meantime the argument has become polarized between those in favor of affirmative action and those opposed to affirmative action. Members of the university community are being forced to join one side or the other in an escalation of this "war fever." Consequently, the problems that affirmative action was designed to meet have been seriously neglected and have moved the college and university campuses toward more violence on campus. Imperfect though it may have been, the need to continue "affirming affirmative action" must be continued (Cheatham, 1991).

As Altbach (1991) points out that race relations are not only a "minority problem" but a concern for everyone in the campus community. Altbach writes that racial issues are apparent in the campus disruptions that have increased recently nationwide.

> More important, racial issues pervade the entire university—from debates about the curriculum to relations in dormitories, from intercollegiate sports to key decisions on admissions. Affirmative action regulations are directly linked to concerns about the representation of racial minorities (as well as women) on the faculties of colleges and universities. Indeed, over the past two decades, racial questions have come to play an unprecedented role in American higher education. (p. 4)

A great number of recent publications deal with the problems of racism on the college and university campus. Green (1989) edited a handbook for the American Council on Education Board of Directors to consider how higher education could take a leadership role in rekindling the nation's commitment to the full participation of minority citizens. Green reviews the literature to examine empirical data on trends in the enrollment and graduation of minority students at the university level, summarizing these trends in eight data-based statements:

1. Higher education's pool of students is increasingly made up of minority youth.
2. College attendance by Black students has slowed; the gap in participation between Whites and Blacks is growing.
3. The rate of college attendance for Hispanic youths has declined in the last decade.

4. College attendance by American Indian students lags far behind Black and Hispanic attendance.
5. Minority students are concentrated in community colleges.
6. Black and Hispanic students are far less likely than White students to complete a degree.
7. Blacks attending historically black colleges and universities (HBCUs) are more likely to complete a degree than those attending predominantly white institutions.
8. Black and Hispanic participation in graduate and professional education can best be described as minuscule in the areas of mathematics and the sciences (Green, 1989, pp. 2-3).

Peterson (1990a) describes how these conditions have led to racial violence on many if not all campuses. "Whatever the causes and whoever may be to blame, a surge of racist expression is clearly washing through American universities right now accompanied by other forms of bigotry, and rooted in a deeper strain of general prejudice that pervades our entire society (p. 45)." Peterson (1990a, 1990b) describes a program at Rutgers to gather data through a needs assessment. With the cooperation of all levels in the university community, a plan was developed. Peterson goes on to describe the problems encountered in applying principles of community psychology to the university community situation in ways that would be very helpful to other universities facing similar problems.

It seems inconsistent for a university to neglect the tools it teaches for solving community problems when attempting to deal with its own problems. If we teach students how to manage conflict, should we not be in a good position to teach ourselves? Should not conflict, such as racial conflict, be handled differently within the university from the way it might be handled in a labor union, in other organizations, or on the street? One traditional method of dealing with problems in the university is debate. Exercise #7 describes how a debate on racial issues might become a useful tool for articulating the issues in a university classroom.

Exercise #7:   A Classroom Debate

Objective:

The process of debating several sides of an issue goes back to the Socratic method and beyond. The basic premise is that if both sides debate the issue vigorously, carefully, and with meticulous regard for the truth, then the right answer to the question under debate will emerge. This exercise is an attempt to apply the methodology of debate to the articulation of racial issues in a classroom setting.

Procedure:

1. A two-sided topic or question is identified regarding ethnic, racial, or cultural issues as they apply to the curriculum in the course for which students are enrolled. For example, one side might emphasize the importance of cultural "similarities" and the other side cultural "differences."
2. Students are divided into two groups and given a week or more to prepare their arguments to debate "their side" of the ethnic, racial, or cultural issue.
3. It is not necessary for the students to actually believe in the point of view they are presenting, although believing in the issue will no doubt enhance their motivation.
4. It is important, however, for students to spend time preparing their arguments and collecting supporting data to present during the debate.
5. The debate between two groups of students will be organized into a sequence of activities to structure the interaction.

Format of the debate:

- Side one gives opening arguments, allowing 3 minutes per member.
- Side two gives opening arguments, allowing 3 minutes per member.
- Side one has 3 minutes for rebuttal and presentation.
- Side two has 3 minutes for rebuttal and presentation.
- Side one has 3 minutes for a second rebuttal and presentation.
- Side two has 3 minutes for a second rebuttal and presentation.
- Side one has 5 minutes to present concluding arguments.
- Side two has 5 minutes to present concluding arguments.

Debriefing:

Following the debate, the other students in the class will score both debating teams to judge the respective merits of each side as presented in the debate. The other class members will use the following scoring criteria for judging the debate with a low score being (1) and a high score being (10):

1. Analytical skill
2. Clarity of argument and position

3. Sophistication of argument
4. Integration of theory and practice
5. Relation of argument to reported research
6. Relation of argument to current events
7. Effective presentation skills
8. General effort expended by the team
9. Innovative and creative ideas
10. Ability to work within the stated time limits

When both teams in the debate have been scored, the facilitator will announce the respective scores of each team as judged by the other students. At that point the class as a whole may want to discuss alternative points of view that were not presented but would have strengthened the argument for one side or the other. The teacher will also want to share notes indicating factual insights and indications of comprehension of the issue demonstrated by both teams during the debate.

Learning Principle:

The classroom provides a safe place to debate risky topics such as racial conflict based on data and empirical evidence and to separate truth from nontruth in the process.

Another way to help students in university classrooms apply their skills to racial problems within the university is through analysis, another traditional method associated with university teaching and learning. Analysis is the process of turning problems into resources; the problems themselves become the textbook. The problems under discussion could be either from within or outside the university structure. The key aspect of analysis is the examination of elements in a complex situation to identify patterns and relationships that make the problem powerful and, ultimately, manageable. Exercise #8 describes how even a brief newspaper article can become a valuable resource for the study of racial conflict.

Exercise #8:   Analysis of a Newspaper Article Through Role Playing

Objective:

Newspapers and media report large numbers of complex situations every day that are both the cause and the effect of racial conflict. These newspaper articles often seem complex in their description of a problem and—if they are well written—suggest no clear or simple solution. By bringing selected newspaper stories into the classroom, it is possible to apply the skills of systematic analysis to the management of even very complex problems. The objective of this exercise is to help students analyze newspaper articles about racial conflict from multiple viewpoints.

Procedure:

1. The teacher or facilitator will select an article from a current newspaper that involves racial conflict either as the cause or the effect of a complicated relationship.

2. Key roles in the newspaper article will be identified, making sure that these roles represent different and contrasting perspectives on the situation being described.

3. Students will be assigned to the various roles identified, either as volunteers or by selection.

4. Students will be given some days to prepare themselves for their roles by becoming more informed about the actual situation and/or by becoming better informed about the population or viewpoint they represent.

5. If necessary, outside resource persons more closely connected with the situation may be brought into the classroom.

6. At an appointed time the students will take on their roles and interact *in character* within the classroom for about 10 or 15 minutes. This role playing can go on for more or less time, depending on the judgment of the facilitator/teacher.

7. Other students in the class will be free to ask questions of the role players who will respond in their roles.

8. The focus of discussion should be on providing a better understanding of the complex situation described in the article from multiple points of view.

Debriefing:

When sufficient data has been gathered describing the same situation from multiple viewpoints, the students will be asked to leave their roles. Each role player will be asked to identify the essential features of this situation of racial conflict from his or her viewpoint. What were the "causes" of the conflict, and what would have to be done to "solve" the problem, which will be noted on the blackboard? When each role player has had an opportunity to report back to the group what she or he learned, the whole class will be asked to discuss (a) how the different viewpoints are different and (b) how the different viewpoints are similar. By analyzing the situation in terms of similarities and differences, the class will be asked to identify the most probable *real* cause and the most likely *actual* solution to the situation.

Learning Principle:

By taking on the roles of participants in racial conflict as reported in a newspaper, it is easier to include both the subjective and the objective elements in analysis to determine appropriate outcome goals in managing the problem.

Planning is another tool taught in university-based classrooms that can be applied to problems of racial conflict. Planning requires accurate information and careful analysis of complex situations. Planning in a multicultural setting also requires the accommodation of contrasting and sometimes contradictory viewpoints or agendas by the different ethnic, racial or cultural groups. While teaching a course on education and society at the University of Malaya some years ago, Pedersen (1991) was told it would be illegal to discuss actual ethnic, racial, and cultural issues in the classroom, but it would not be illegal to discuss those issues in a simulation of a society much like Malaysia. As a result, Exercise #9 emerged, where complex situations involving racial conflict were adapted to a board game designed by groups of students in different ethnic, racial, or cultural roles.

Exercise #9:   Designing a Multiethnic Simulation

Objective:

Designing a simulation of multiethnic groups interacting together will increase the student's knowledge about the contrasting viewpoints of each ethnic/racial group and the unique advantages or disadvantages of membership in each group. The simulation will provide a "safe" setting to discuss "risky" topics of how different ethnic, racial, or cultural groups interact and manage conflict with one another.

Procedure:

1. Students will be organized into planning groups of six who will work together in contrasting roles to design the simulation.

2. A game board will be provided to each group resembling the game board for *Monopoly*, although the spaces around the perimeter of the board will be blank and no game rules or instructions will be provided.

3. Each of the six members will take on the role of a different ethnic, racial, or cultural group, with three of those roles being low-income members of that group and three being high-income members. Each group will determine the appropriate ethnic, racial, or cultural group identity with the teacher/facilitator.

4. Each group will establish a problem situation in which members of their different cultures would be likely to interact, such as a week in a school or university, a 3-day jury session in a trial setting, a month-long series of committee meetings on a community development project, or some other complex multicultural situation.

5. The 30 or 40 empty cells surrounding the game board will each be identified as an "event" that would be likely to occur within the larger complex situation.

6. Each participating student will then identify the specific advantages or disadvantages of each event for persons from their ethnic, racial, cultural group and income level. There will essentially be six sets of rules, with different rules for each participant.

7. Students will be encouraged to research the viewpoint of their group to make the consequences of each event as realistic as possible.

8. Currency will be distributed to participants, with twice as much currency being distributed to the high-income as to the low-income players. Each event will have consequences resulting in the increase or decrease of resources for the player.

9. The game is then played with each player given a marker and the movement of markers being determined by dice.

Debriefing:

The game must be playable. The game should also result in players becoming more familiar with the advantages and disadvantages of persons from different ethnic, racial, and cultural groups who compete and cooperate with one another in the same situation. By establishing specific events, the players will have analyzed the components within a complex situation and the consequences of each event for each group. Discussion following the design of this simulation might include questions such as:

- Does each group have the same ultimate goal such as money, influence, popularity, or power?
- Does each group interact with the same amount of resources in terms of money, power, or opportunity?

- What are the policy objectives for each group, and how are those objectives similar or different?
- What would be the appropriate criteria for "winning" this game?
- How large a role is played by chance and how much is determined by skill?
- What did the players learn about the culture they represented that they did not know before?
- What can be learned from this simulation that would apply to racial conflict in society between and among ethnic, racial, and cultural groups?

Learning Principle:

There are specific advantages and disadvantages for members of each ethnic, racial, or cultural group as they interact in complex social situations.

Most racial conflict involves competition for limited resources. If you want to see the *real* priorities in an organization, you will find a much clearer ranking of priorities in that organization's budget and allocation of resources than in the rhetoric about what they presume to represent. Consequently it is important to look at negotiation as still another approach to problem solving that is taught at the university level and can usefully be applied to the study of conflict between ethnic, racial, and cultural groups. By examining the process of negotiation in a simulated budget dispute it will be possible to study both the *process* of how these different groups negotiate with one another and the *content* of their various arguments for or against budget allocations. Exercise #10 was developed by Drs. Marshal Singer and Paul Pedersen to look at the processes of competition and cooperation in a multicultural society.

Exercise #10:   Lump Sum

Objective:

By simulating a gathering of different ethnic, racial, and cultural groups with contrasting or competing agendas as they seek consensus, it is possible to get a better understanding of the negotiation process in a multicultural setting. The need to reach consensus competes with the need to remain faithful to the best interests of one's ethnic, racial, or cultural group. The fragility of consensus in a multicultural group becomes apparent.

Procedure:

1. A group of students ranging in size from 16 to 60 or so is assembled for a simulation on multicultural issues.

2. Once assembled, the larger group is divided, either arbitrarily or by assignment, into four to six constituencies, so that each constituency has a minimum of four members. For example, the constituent groups may be representatives of ethnic groups in a community, subdivisions of an organization, states in a region, country areas in an international association or branches of a company. The constituent groups are selected to represent a real-world group of special interest to the students, to demonstrate contrasting ethnic, racial, or cultural group memberships, and to be a group about which students can learn either through personal contact or published materials.

3. Once the students are members of their constituent groups, an announcement is made that they have been assembled to decide on the allocation of a large sum of money (usually $1 million to $10 million is about right) by the United Nations. This money must be allocated within the next 2 hours or it will revert to the General Fund. The only requirement that the United Nations places on the allocation decision is that it must be by consensus and total agreement of all groups.

4. Each constituent group is instructed to elect a negotiator (by majority rule voting), decide on the overall division of funds, prepare an argument in support of their allocation, and design bargaining strategies to secure the cooperation of other groups in achieving consensus within the time limit. The group is given *20 minutes* for this first planning session.

5. At the end of the first planning session each group will send a negotiator to a table in the center of the groups. Each negotiator will be given *3 minutes* to present his or her group's plan for how the total amount of money should be allocated, presenting the rationale for this division of funds. There will be no discussion during this first presentation.

6. When all negotiators have made their presentations the negotiators will return to their special interest groups for *10 minutes* to consult with their own group members and members of other groups about modifying their plans, strategies, and tactics.

7. When the second planning session is completed, each group will send a negotiator to the negotiation table for a second *10 minute* negotiation session where each negotiator will seek to present a modified plan, strategy, or tactic based on their discussions with members of their own group or other groups.

8. Following the negotiation session, the groups will return to their groups for another *10 minutes* to discuss further modifications to their plan for allocating funds.

9. The final negotiation session will allow *20 minutes* for the negotiators to assemble and negotiate with one another to achieve consensus. If the negotiators do not reach unanimous agreement before the 20 minutes have expired, the facilitator will announce that they have lost the money, which will now be returned to the United Nations General Fund.

Debriefing:

Whether the group reaches consensus or not, the session should be followed by at least 20 minutes of debriefing about insights gained through the simulation. Discussion may include the factual content information which members learned about their own or other ethnic, racial, or cultural groups through the discussion. Discussion may also include what the participants learned regarding the process of negotiating in a multicultural group for limited resources. Some of the factors that might have contributed toward either achieving or not achieving consensus might be:

- Stubbornness of one or two individuals
- Group pressure not to give in
- Generalized fear of compromising principles for the sake of money
- Indifference about the simulation experience
- A desire to alienate other individuals in other groups
- Disharmony among participants prior to the simulation exercise
- Misguided and unskilled negotiators
- Perception that role authenticity would prevent compromise
- A tendency in the final bargaining sessions to ignore the money and stick to one's principles
- Failure to consider—or having considered, rejection of the alternative—to set up a special fund for allocating the money among interest groups at a later date
- Domination of the simulation by one or two interest groups
- Loyalty to the interest group
- Personal self-interest of one or more groups holding out for too much money
- Stubbornness of one or more groups
- Instructor's guidance and direction
- Negotiators functioning as a sub-group independent of their constituent groups.

Learning Principle:

The relative importance for successful negotiations of tangible goals such as money and intangible goals such as ideals and principles, becomes apparent among different ethnic, racial, and cultural groups.

Chapter Summary

This chapter has emphasized the importance of knowledge or comprehension of culturally relevant information as an intermediate stage of developing multicultural awareness. The various exercises presented build on the awareness exercises in the previous chapter that describe a beginning stage of developing multicultural awareness. The utility of tools appropriate to college- and university-level educational activities, such as negotiation, analysis, debate, and planning, have been illustrated in the exercises of this chapter. In this way, university students can apply the tools they are learning in the classroom for a better understanding of ethnic racial and cultural differences in the university itself.

There are many ways in which racial conflict can be solved. Some of them involve violence and the overthrow of one group by another or the forceful domination of a more powerful ethnic, racial, or cultural group over competing groups. Of all the alternatives, education provides the most attractive choice as the least expensive and potentially the most effective in bringing about long-term harmony. In spite of this, the violent solutions to racial conflict continue to be popular and to consume a disproportionately large amount of the nation's resources. In an age where it is cheaper to send a person to Harvard than to prison, we are past the time of decision. If education is to succeed in dealing with racial conflict and in bringing about harmony in our multicultural world, these issues must be dealt with in our schools and universities. If schools and universities are unable to deal with racial conflict in their own organizations, then how will they be able to prepare students to deal with racial conflict in the outside world?

9

Race Relations in the Community

The last two chapters have dealt with developing an awareness and a knowledge of culturally learned patterns that may facilitate or prevent prejudice and conflict between ethnic, racial, and cultural groups. This chapter will focus on the skills necessary to take appropriate action in prejudice prevention. Skill learning is the most important of the three levels in multicultural development and requires a solid foundation of cultural awareness and knowledge.

It is important, for example, to be both aware and knowledgeable about a particular group's preferred method of receiving help before intruding. A community group will be much more ready to learn from you if you have allowed them to teach you about themselves first. Because problems are similar across cultures, it is easy to assume that the solutions to those problems will also be similar. However, the appropriate response to problems is almost always culturally unique, and one's "self-reference criterion" will almost certainly betray the unsuspecting counselor.

Multicultural counseling is not just working with exotic populations. From a world-wide numerical perspective, the most familiar definitions of *culture* are themselves exotic. It is important, therefore, to understand multicultural counseling as both complex—involving some aspects of all counseling relationships—and dynamic—focused on the rapidly changing salience from one culture to another (Pedersen, 1988). Cross (1991) emphasizes the importance of salience in the development of an ethnic, racial or cultural identity, even at the highest "internalization" fifth stage of identity development. "While advanced Black identity development results in one's giving high salience to issues of race and culture, not every person in the Internalization stage shares the same degree of salience for Blackness, as this is likely to be determined by the nature of one's ideology (p. 212)."

In our attempt to apply counseling across cultures we have made several errors. The first error has been to overemphasize the importance of a person's behavior and underemphasize the importance of the culturally learned expectations and values that give the behaviors meaning. Interpreting behaviors categorically and independently has frequently resulted in naively imposing narrowly defined criteria for "normal behavior" as defined by the more powerful culture on a culturally diverse client population.

A second error is to oversimplify the social systems relevant to the counseling situation by focusing exclusively on the most obvious "culture" to which a client may belong, whether that more obvious category is ethnicity, gender, age, socioeconomic status, disability, or membership in a particular organization. Wrenn (1962, 1985) wrote extensively about the dangers of cultural encapsulation by counselors who overemphasize technique-oriented approaches to counseling and disregard cultural differences between clients and counselors.

A third error that is most apparent in the counseling literature limits counseling to a formal process taking place in a formal setting. Kleinman (1980) contrasts this specialized perspective of counseling, which is focused on the "disease" or the malfunctioning unit in an almost mechanistic way, to an alternative systems approach, which is focused on the "illness" a person is experiencing and the many different ways that condition is requiring the person to change. In many—if not most—cultures, the preferred context for receiving help may be in an informal or less formal setting than the counselor's "office." In a similar mode, the most preferable method for helping may be through presentations, support groups, advice-giving, or even family friendship (see recent discussion by Atkinson, Thompson, & Grant, 1993).

Intervention into another culture is most frequently judged by the relevance of that intervention from the receiving culture's viewpoint. The intervention must be judged practical, otherwise the counselor will be guilty of "scratching where it doesn't itch." Problem situations in the host culture can, therefore, become valuable training resources for both understanding and intervention. The "critical incident" methodology collects examples of problem situations in the host culture that have no easy answers, project serious consequences, and have occurred in a very short

(3 to 5 minute) period of time. Critical incidents are similar to brief case studies but differ in their more limited focus on specific aspects.

There is no substitute for real experience. The critical incident technique is an attempt to bring actual experiences or events into the classroom as a resource. The incident is "critical" meaning important, essential or valuable, in the way that a part of a machine might be critical to the smooth operation of the machine. The incident is a short description of an event that did or could take place in a 5- or 10-minute period of time. A case study, by contrast, is much more complicated and might take place over weeks, months, or even years.

Critical incidents are based on real-life situations and typically involve a "dilemma" where there is no easy or obvious solution. The objective of critical incidents is to stimulate thinking about basic and important issues that occur in real life. By reviewing the incident, participants can imagine themselves in the same situation, develop strategies to deal with that situation, and become more realistic in their expectations. Rehearsing what a participant would do in a critical incident in the relative safety of a training situation requires limited risk-taking and yet provides much of the complexity of real-life situations.

Critical incidents do not necessarily imply a single solution or "right way" of resolving the dilemma in the situation. Instead, they allow participants to explore alternative solutions and their implications. Exercise 11 describes the use of critical incidents for appropriate intervention in ethnic, racial, or culturally different communities.

Exercise #11:   Critical Incidents

Objective:

By taking a "slice-of-life" critical incident example and studying it in depth, participants will become better able to identify the culturally accurate causes and culturally appropriate responses to the situation. By examining the alternative responses to each situation and the different consequences of each alternative, it will become possible to generalize patterns from the critical incident that apply to other situations in that host culture. The critical incident becomes a "window" into the host culture. Focusing on actual incidents also ensures the practicality of this activity, keeping in touch with situations as they actually exist. Finally, critical incidents are valuable in preserving the inherent complexity of each multicultural situation without oversimplification. Some of the alternative skill-building exercises have the danger of oversimplifying cultures in ways that make generalization to the real world very difficult.

Procedure:

1. Collect examples of "critical incident" problem situations in a target host culture that have no easy answers, involve serious consequences, and occur with some frequency. If at all possible, it would be particularly useful if the students themselves collected the critical incidents.
   a. The critical incident format will typically include the following components:
   b. Identify the event or occurrence with as much specificity as possible: the problem to be solved, the issue involved, and so on.
   c. Describe the relevant details and circumstances surrounding the event, so that readers will understand what happened.
   d. List the people involved and describe them and their relationships to you and to one another.
   e. Describe your own role in the situation, that is, what you did and how you acted, and identify the particular cross-cultural skill or skills involved. What were your other choices and how would you do things differently next time?
   f. Write a brief analysis of the incident, telling what you learned from the experience. State your estimate of the level of development of your particular cross-cultural skills as you reflect on the incident.
   g. Identify the specific psychological construct or concept from the class readings or discussion that is illustrated by the dynamics of this critical incident.
2. Divide participants into small, five-person groups to discuss the alternatives to each critical incident and the consequences of each alternative. All groups may work independently on the same critical incident and compare their findings, or the groups may work on different critical incidents to search for culturally learned patterns across situations. It may be useful to role play the brief situation as well as discuss it to understand better the dynamics of relationships.
3. Wherever possible, it would be useful to have resource persons from the culture or cultures involved in the situation assist in presenting the incident to the group or groups.
4. In addition to identifying alternative responses and the consequences of each response to the situation, the group or groups may be given additional tasks, such as separating the cultural from the personal element, identifying specific barriers to communication, or identifying the feelings that different persons in the situation might have had as a result of the critical incident.

5. After about 30 minutes of discussion ask each group to report their findings and conclusions back to the total group. Defer discussion by the total group until all groups have reported back in order to avoid repetition and to identify patterns across situations.
6. The small group reports might be judged according to specific objectives and scored by other participants for later discussion.

Debriefing:

There are several ways in which the participants can be debriefed on their analysis of critical incidents. Critical incidents can be useful in many ways:

*   The ability to use many information sources within a social or cultural environment may be increased. The student should work to develop information-gathering skills such as observing, questioning, and listening carefully.
*   Awareness and understanding of the values, feelings, and attitudes of people in another culture and why they behave as they do should be heightened.
*   Listening well and speaking clearly to both the verbal and nonverbal messages will be recognized as important skills for interpreting physical movements, facial expressions, and the whole range of meanings conveyed in face-to-face encounters.
*   Enhanced ability to become involved with people from other cultures may be developed through collecting and analyzing critical incidents. This process involves giving and inspiring trust and confidence and developing a basis for mutual liking or respect. Students may learn ways to be both truthful and sensitive to the feelings of others.
*   The ability to reach conclusions based on assessment of limited data is also an important skill. This form of problem solving requires a systematic approach that will identify cultural salience even as it changes from moment to moment.

Learning Principle:

Problems can become useful resources for learning about culturally complex patterns of an ethnic, racial, or cultural group.

The Complexity of Culture

There are many different ways culture is defined. Sometimes *culture* refers to visible or "point-at-able" (Hines & Pedersen, 1980) artifacts or behaviors that are culturally learned and that can be objectively identified or pointed at by both persons within and outside the group. Another definition refers to *subjective culture*, defined by internalized feelings, attitudes, opinions, and assumptions that members of a group consider to be profoundly important. Because this definition is subjective, it is difficult to verify (Triandis, Vassiliou, Vassiliou, Tanaka, & Shanmugam, 1972). Another polarity of definitions contrasts a narrow definition of culture with a broad definition of culture. The narrow definition of culture is limited almost totally to anthropological descriptors such as nationality and ethnicity. A broader social-systems definition of culture includes demographic variables, such as age, gender, and place of residence; status variables, such as social, educational, and economic level; and affiliation variables to formal and/or informal groups, in addition to ethnographic variables of nationality ethnicity, religion, and language (Hines & Pedersen, 1980).

Still a third polarity contrasts an emphasis on culture-specific with culture-general perspectives. The culture-specific perspective limits the definition to multiethnic or multinational analysis and is mostly a method for helping people learn about or compare different specific groups defined by nationality or ethnicity. An overemphasis on the specific perspective results in politicized and somewhat stereotyped categories that ignore within-group differences. The culture-general perspective presumes that cultural differences are not important and that the best interests of society require us to emphasize only the ways we are all the same. An overemphasis on the culture-general approach results in the "melting pot" myth and exploitation of less powerful groups by more powerful groups. The more accurate perspective emphasizes *both* the culture specific *and* the culture general perspective at the same time. "Just as differentiation and integration are complementary processes, so are the emic (culture-specific) and the etic (culture-general) perspectives necessarily interrelated" (Pedersen, 1991, p. 7).

Culture can be defined as within the person rather than within the group. If culture is indeed within the person, then an essential part of personality development includes multicultural identity development. This perspective goes beyond the obvious labels used to describe individual groups and collections of groups. The broad definition of culture emphasizes the process of developing a multicultural identity as complex and contextual rather than simple. The subjective definition of culture emphasizes its dynamic and elusive character as the salience changes from one focus to another. In the development of multicultural awareness, knowledge, and skill, it is important to form a clear and accurate picture of a one's multicultural identity as the first step to shaping and influencing one's multicultural environment, bringing about desired changes, and comprehending the meaning of culture.

One means of charting both the *intracultural* ways that culture functions within the person and the *intercultural* ways that culture functions between persons is called the Cultural Grid. The Cultural Grid is based on the premise that culture is within the person and not within the group. This model was developed to identify and describe the linkage between behavior, expectations, values, and social system variables for a particular decision at a particular point in time. The Cultural Grid combines social system variables on one dimension and personal variables on the other dimension. Rather than describing a person's culture in the abstract, the Cultural Grid matches a specific decision or behavior to the specific expectations behind that behavior, to the specific values behind the expectation to the specific social system variables where those values were learned. Culture is complex (linked to a great many expectations and values) and dynamic (learned from a great many different social systems) but not chaotic.

Each behavior is given meaning by referring to the expectations and values behind that behavior. Behavior by itself is not data but meaningless noise. It is only through reference to cultural learned expectations and values that specific behaviors take on meaning. Exercise 12 will demonstrate how a specific behavior can be analyzed using the *intrapersonal* Cultural Grid.

Exercise #12:   The Intrapersonal Cultural Grid

Objective:

The visual representation of an individual's personal cultural orientation, with social system variables of ethnographic, demographic, status, and affiliation on one dimension and personal variables of behavior, expectation, and value on the other dimension, helps to organize the culture within the person. This Cultural Grid will help individuals understand how culture influences and shapes each specific behavior. Behavior is defined as a specific, identifiable action by an individual. Expectation is defined as a cognitive variable that includes behavior-outcome and stimulus-outcome expectancies that guide the individual's choice of behavior. Values are the belief systems that explain the importance of expectations. Social system variables are the sources of understanding or the "teachers" in society from which the values were learned.

Procedure:

1. Distribute blank copies of an intrapersonal cultural grid to all participants. The framework will look as follows:

Social System Variables	Behavior	Expectation	Value
Ethnographic			
Nationality			
Ethnicity			
Language			
Religion			
Demographic			
Age			
Gender			
Place of residence			
Status			
Social			
Educational			
Economic			
Affiliation			
Formal groups			
Informal groups			

2. The analysis begins by identifying a specific behavior, such as the decision to read this book. Ask all members of the group to analyze the same behavior, whatever that specific behavior may be.

3. Ask participants to identify as many expectations behind that behavior as they can, focusing on the two or three that are most important and listing them under the Expectation column on the chart. For example, "If I read this book, then I can expect to learn a new approach to preventing prejudice." The expected consequences are what lead the individual to perform a particular behavior. Each specific behavior is linked to many different expectations.

4. Ask participants to identify as many values behind each expectation as they can, focusing on the two or three that are most important and listing them under the Values column on the chart. For example "Learning new approaches to prevent prejudice is important because I value learning." Each expectation is grounded in many different values.

5. Ask participants to identify the social system variables that taught them the particular values they have already listed. The values were learned from a variety of sources in society indicated in the categories of the Social System

variables. For example, the value "Learning" may be rooted in one's ethnic heritage, one's age group, specific social-economic-educational peer groups, family, organizations or support groups. Check which Social System Variables were most important in teaching the identified values. Each value will be rooted in many different social system variables.

6. Each person should be given about fifteen minutes to complete a personal-cultural Intrapersonal Cultural Grid.

7. Discuss the linkages among a particular behavior, the expectations behind that behavior, and the values behind the expectations, as well as the social system variables behind the values.

Debriefing:

The Intrapersonal Cultural Grid is frozen in time and gives a glimpse of how culture shapes a particular behavior only for that frozen moment. Culture is dynamic and the combination of variables will change from time to time and place to place as well as from person to person. Compare and contrast how different members of the group displayed the same behavior but had different expectations and values. Compare and contrast the different social systems variables that taught different persons the same value or values. Discuss how the Cultural Grid provides an accurate and comprehensive assessment of a specific behavior relative to that person's cultural background. Discuss how dangerous it would be to interpret behavior without reference to culturally learned expectations and values. Discuss how including culture in the analysis results in a more accurate comprehension of the behavior. Discuss how the same behavior might have different meanings while different behaviors might have the same meaning.

Learning Principle:

Behavior is not data until and unless it is linked to culturally learned expectations and values.

The Cultural Grid is also useful in understanding the interactions between two or more culturally different individuals in an *interpersonal* Cultural Grid. If two persons interpret one another's behavior without reference to culturally learned expectations and values that interpretation is certain to be inaccurate. Similar behaviors may have different meanings and different behaviors might have the same meaning, as indicated on the Intrapersonal Cultural Grid. If we extend that insight to the analysis of differences between persons it is easy to see the extreme importance of judging each behavior according to the expectations and values behind those behaviors between persons (A. Pedersen & P. Pedersen, 1989; P. Pedersen & A. Pedersen, 1989). If two persons are accurate in their interpretations of one another's behavior and they know it, they do not always need to display the same behavior. The two people may agree to disagree about what behavior is appropriate and still work together in harmony.

For example, think of your very best friend in the world. It will usually be true that your "best friends" behave in different ways from you and very different from behavior you would "accept" from strangers. Why do you accept that behavior from your best friend? Perhaps because you interpret the different or unacceptable behavior in the context of shared "friendship." Those dissimilar behaviors are not problematical (and may actually enhance the quality of the relationship) because of the similar expectation of friendship shared by both persons.

This same principle can be applied to the relationships between any two culturally different people, especially when they share the same expectations and values, even though they may behave quite differently. Exercise 13 describes the *interpersonal* Cultural Grid to show how one might analyze differences and similarities across cultures accurately.

Exercise #13:   The Interpersonal Cultural Grid

Objective:

The interpersonal Cultural Grid provides a conceptual road map for the accurate interpretation of a culturally different person's behavior in the context of that person's culturally learned expectations. The exercise shows that it is not necessary for two persons to share the same behaviors as long as they share the same positive expectations. The Cultural Grid analyzes behavior both within persons and between persons, providing practical assistance in managing the complexity of intercultural conflict. There are several ways that this Cultural Grid can be used.

- The Cultural Grid provides a framework to separate the personal from the cultural aspects of an interaction.
- Personal-cultural orientations can be compared across time and across people to show how the same behavior can be explained by different expectations or values in different cultural settings.
- The dynamic and changing salience of social system variables are matched with personal-cultural variables for each time and place and person.

- A comprehensively broad description of culture provides the opportunity to consider all sources of culturally learned patterns.
- The culture-specific variable of behavior differences is combined with the culture-general variable of similarities in expectations and values showing how both the specific and the general perspectives complement one another.

Procedure:

1. Identify an example of conflict between two persons from different cultures for analysis using the Interpersonal Cultural Grid.
2. Divide the participants into small groups of two to five persons working together to analyze the conflict using the Grid.
3. Distribute work sheets in which the four quadrants of the Interpersonal Cultural Grid are drawn as follows:

Behaviors

	Same	Different
Same	I	II
Different	III	IV

Expectations (row label at left: Same / Different)

4. Each team will identify examples in the first quadrant where the two culturally different individuals have similar behaviors and similar positive expectations. Both persons expect friendliness and both persons smile. There is a high level of accuracy in both person's interpretation of one another's behavior. This aspect of the relationship would indicate intercultural harmony.
5. Each team will identify examples in the second quadrant where the two culturally different individuals have different behaviors but share the same positive expectation. Both persons expect friendliness but only one person is smiling. This part of the relationship is characteristic of intercultural conflict where each person is applying a "self-reference criterion" to interpret the other person's behavior in terms of the self-reference expectations and values.
6. Each team will identify examples in the third quadrant where the two culturally different individuals have the same behaviors but now have different and/or negative expectations. For example, both are smiling but only one expects friendship. The two persons may appear friendly to one another but actually be in serious conflict because their expectations are different and/or negative.

7. Each team will identify examples in the fourth quadrant where the two culturally different individuals have different behaviors and different or negative
expectations as well. Not only do they disagree in their behaviors toward
one another but now they also openly disagree on their expectations for the
future. This relationship is likely to result in hostile disengagement.

8. The teams will now discuss how they can keep the conflict in quadrant two
from moving to quadrant three and/or four by emphasizing the shared and
positive expectations between the two culturally different individuals and
by not being distracted by culturally different behaviors.

Debriefing:

Smiling is an ambiguous behavior. It may or may not imply trust and
friendliness. The smile may or may not be interpreted accurately. Outside
its culturally learned context the smile has no fixed meaning. Two persons
with similar expectations for friendliness may not both be smiling. The
salience of intercultural conflict is likely to move from quadrant one to
quadrant two to quadrant three and finally to quadrant four unless a skilled
facilitator intervenes.

Two persons look forward to working together (quadrant one). While
both persons expect FRIENDLINESS, one person shows that by behaving
FORMALLY while the other person shows that by behaving INFORMALLY
(quadrant two). If they are distracted by the behavior, then the less powerful
of the two will probably adjust behavior to fit the behavior of the more
powerful. Now they have the same behavior, but the less powerful member is expecting UNFRIENDLY while the more powerful person might
still expect FRIENDLY (quadrant three). Finally, the less powerful person
becomes fed up with compromising his or her values by pretending to
show friendliness, and the two persons separate in anger (quadrant four).

If, on the other hand, the two people are able to discuss in quadrant two
that their behaviors might be very different but their expectations are very
similar, the relationship can be salvaged without either person having to
change or modify behaviors—as long as there are shared and positive
expectations on which they can build the relationship. The debriefing
discussion would look at the importance of shared expectations in the
critical incident under discussion and discuss how that potentially conflictual relationship can be salvaged by emphasizing similarities of positive expectation and de-emphasizing differences of behavior.

Learning Principle:

An accurate assessment of interpersonal relationships across cultures must assess both persons' behaviors in the context of their culturally learned expectations and values.

The *intrapersonal* and the *interpersonal* Cultural Grids provide tools for understanding how culture is related to behavior and suggest specific procedures for reducing conflict between culturally different persons. There are four steps to applying the Cultural Grid in practice.

1. Identify one or more specific behaviors of an individual or conflicting behaviors among several individuals from different cultural backgrounds.
2. Identify the positive expectation which each person might potentially attach to the behavior or behaviors. What is expected to happen as a result of that behavior? Each behavior will probably have several positive (at least as perceived by the person him or her self) expectations.
3. Identify the values that each person attaches to the culturally learned positive expectation. What are the underlying values in which that positive expectation is grounded? What is the meaning and importance of that expectation for the person?
4. Identify the social system variables where those values have been taught to the person or persons so that you can better understand the basis for the cultural values that led to expectations that led to the behavior.

Chapter Summary

This chapter has discussed skills for preventing prejudice in the community. The emphasis has been on looking at critical incidents or "slices of life" to capture the complexity of culture in a real life context. The emphasis furthermore has been on looking beyond the different behaviors displayed by culturally different persons to search for shared expectations and values. It is only when this area of "common ground" has been identified that two culturally different persons are likely to work together in harmony. If we are to survive in a culturally different and diverse future world it will be important for us to learn how those cultural differences can become positive rather than negative forces in our lives. That achievement will indicate the highest level of ethnic, racial, or cultural identity development.

PART IV

Prejudice Prevention: Assessment, Research, and Resources

The final section of *Preventing Prejudice* includes two chapters. Chapter 10 reviews instruments designed to measure racism and discrimination, racial identity levels, and multicultural counseling awareness. Guidelines for using instrumentation are presented, and the importance of evaluation and accountability in prejudice-prevention programming is highlighted. The final chapter in the book is organized as a mini-resource guide for counselors and educators looking for sources on the topic. Here it is stressed that *how* the resources are used is more important than *what* resources are used.

10

Assessment of Prejudice and Racial Identity

As counselors continue to work in the prejudice-prevention area, and, in fact, as they increase their activities in this critical arena, a strong need arises for assessment devices to assist them in their work. Assessments are needed to help counselors measure their constructs of interest (e.g., racism and prejudice, discrimination, racial identity, and multicultural counseling awareness) and to evaluate the effectiveness of their interventions.

Each year in the United States hundreds of lectures, workshops, and seminars on multiculturalism are provided to students and educators, yet few of these programs include objective evaluation components. Counselors have a professional and ethical responsibility (see Ponterotto, 1991) to assess their own competence in the multicultural area and to evaluate the effectiveness of their interventions. This chapter briefly reviews paper-and-pencil instruments that counselors can incorporate into their multicultural practice and research.

The three categories of instruments this chapter focuses on are: racism and prejudice, racial identity/consciousness development, and multicultural counseling competence. These instruments can be completed by the reader to assess her or his own levels of race/gender bias, racial identity, or specific multicultural counseling competency levels. They also can be used by counselors in their day-to-day teaching, consulting and counseling work. A common use of the instruments, particularly the prejudice and counseling competency scales, is as a pre-post measure before and after some intervention (e.g., a workshop, or semester course). Two of the instruments reviewed in this chapter, along with scoring directions, are presented in the Appendices. We caution the reader that the descriptions in this chapter are very brief and designed simply to introduce the reader to multicultural measurement. To request copies of instruments and to receive detailed psychometric, scoring, and administration guidelines, the reader should read the references cited and contact the respective instrument developers.

Racism and Prejudice Instruments

Modern Racism Scale

The Modern Racism Scale (MRS; McConahay, 1986) is designed to measure White people's racial attitudes toward Blacks. The MRS is a brief instrument, consisting of six or seven items (depending on the target population). Each item is worded along a 4-point or 5-point Likert-type format. The brevity of the MRS makes it easy to administer and score. An example of an MRS item is as follows: "Over the past few years, the government and news media have shown more respect to Blacks than they deserve" (Sabnani & Ponterotto, 1992, p. 171).

A recent psychometric review of the MRS (Sabnani & Ponterotto, 1992) reported the instrument to have satisfactory internal consistency, with coefficient alphas (the preferred internal consistency measure, see Ponterotto & Furlong, 1985) ranging from .75 to .86 across a number of large samples. The MRS is fairly stable over short periods of time, with test-retest stability results ranging from .72 to .93 across numerous samples. The MRS has also demonstrated varying degrees of construct and convergent validity. For additional information on the MRS and for the address of its author, see McConahay (1983, 1986). For a modified version of the MRS, see Jacobson's (1985) New Racism Scale.

Institutional Racism Scale

The Institutional Racism Scale (IRS) was developed to assess ". . . how individuals construe institutional racism, engage in anti-racism, and view organizational commitment to the reduction of racism" (Barbarin & Gilbert, 1981, p. 147). The IRS is a carefully thought out and constructed instrument. It is composed of six subscales: Indices of Racism (8 Likert-type items), Effectiveness of Strategies to Reduce Racism (11 Likert-type items), Extent of the Use of Strategies (7 Likert-type items), Agency Climate for Racism (6 Likert-type items), Administrative Efforts to Reduce Racism (20 semantic differential items), and Personal Efforts to Reduce Racism (20 semantic differential items). In total, the IRS consists of 72 items.

Barbarin and Gilbert (1981) report internal consistency (using the Kuder-Richardson-14 formula) results for the various IRS subscales ranging from .69 to .94. These consistency measures are satisfactory. Stability of the IRS as measured by test-retest reliability over a 2-month period ranged from .55 to .79 across subscales. It appears that the IRS is moderately stable over short periods of time. Barbarin and Gilbert (1981) also present some evidence of the instrument's concurrent validity.

Situational Attitude Scale

The Situational Attitude Scale (SAS; Sedlacek & Brooks, 1970) was originally designed to measure attitudes of Whites toward Blacks in various social and personal contexts. The SAS presents ten interpersonal scenarios, each of which is followed by 10 five-point bipolar semantic differential scales (e.g., happy. . . sad). In total, there are 100 items on the SAS. A sample scenario reads: "You meet your new roommate" (the neutral condition), and "You meet your new roommate who is Black" (the race condition). Another scenario reads: "Your best friend has just become engaged" (neutral condition), and "Your best friend has just become engaged to a Black person" (race condition) (White & Sedlacek, 1987, p. 183).

The SAS has been used extensively in student development research, particularly by William Sedlacek of the University of Maryland. The instrument has satisfactory internal consistency, with reliability coefficients ranging from .64 to .90 across numerous samples (see Balanger, Hoffman, & Sedlacek, 1992; White & Sedlacek, 1987). The SAS has been modified for use in attitude measurement regarding women, male sex roles, persons with disabilities, and children.

Quick Discrimination Index

The Quick Discrimination Index (QDI) is a new paper-and-pencil instrument designed to measure subtle racial prejudice and sexism (Ponterotto et al., 1993). The QDI consists of 25 items placed on a 5-point Likert-type scale. The total score ranges from 25 (low sensitivity to race- and gender-issues; prejudiced and sexist) to 125 (extremely sensitive and aware of race and gender issues; prejudice-free and nonracist). Ponterotto et al. (1993) developed the QDI to fill the perceived need for a more subtle measure of prejudice and sexism. The authors believed that many of the existing instruments included items that were easily discernible as prejudice measures and therefore subject to social desirability contamination. In other words, there is concern that respondents answer the items in a socially acceptable way rather than in a way that accurately reflects their thoughts and feelings. The QDI addresses this concern using very careful wording and measuring the constructs in a very subtle manner.

Appendix I presents the complete QDI, along with directions for scoring the instrument. The reader will note that the instrument is actually titled the Social Attitude Survey so as to control for initial respondent reactivity. To prevent response bias, a number of QDI items are reverse-worded and therefore must be scored in reverse when tallying instrument total scores.

The QDI is still undergoing psychometric validation, but initial data appears promising. The instrument has adequate internal consistency, with a coefficient alpha of .89 for a heterogeneous development sample. The instrument has also demonstrated criterion-related validity by successfully predicting differences in group scores (see Ponterotto et al., 1993 for full details).

Racial Identity Attitude Instruments

Black Racial Identity/Consciousness

Three self-report instruments designed to measure Black racial identity or "Black consciousness" are the African Self-Consciousness Scale (ASCS; Baldwin & Bell, 1985), the Developmental Inventory of Black Consciousness (DIB-C; Milliones, 1980), and the Racial Identity Attitude Scale (RIAS: Parham & Helms, 1981; Helms, 1990b). The ASCS includes 42 Likert-type items. The instrument has good test-retest reliability and satisfactory content- and convergent-validity. The DIB-C consists of 65 Likert-type items. Although there has not been much psychometric research on the DIB-C to date, the few available studies indicate that the instrument has fair to moderate levels of construct- and convergent-validity. Much more validation research on both the DIB-C and the ASCS is needed before counselors can use the instruments with confidence.

The Racial Identity Attitude Scale (RIAS) is by far the most utilized and researched Black racial identity instrument. The RIAS is a multidimensional instrument measuring attitudes consistent with William Cross's stages of Black racial identity (see Chapter 4). There are two short versions of the RIAS (each with 30 Likert-type items), and one longer version (50 Likert-type items). Most of the research has utilized a short version of the instrument. Psychometrically, the RIAS has been found to have fair-to-good internal consistency, and moderate construct- and convergent-validity. An extensive psychometric critique of the three identity instruments provided here as well as other minority-focused instrumentation, was recently provided by Sabnani and Ponterotto (1992). To view the instruments themselves and/or to secure the developers' addresses to request permission to use the instruments, see the original references cited above (see Helms, 1990b).

White Racial Identity/Consciousness

The objective measurement of White racial identity attitudes has only recently begun to receive systematic attention in the research literature. Presently, the White Racial Identity Attitude Scale (WRIAS; Helms, 1990b) is the only widely used instrument in this category. (Note: Initial work on related instruments is being conducted by Claney and Parker [1989] and Evans and Ochs [1991]). The WRIAS is a multidimensional instrument measuring attitudes consistent with Helms's White identity stages (see Chapter 5). The instrument appears to have fair to satisfactory internal onsistency as well as moderate evidence for construct- and convergent-validity.

Multicultural Counseling Competency Instruments

One important theme of this book is that if counselors are to intervene effectively in the area of prejudice prevention, they must first be sensitive to and knowledgeable about multicultural issues. For decades, counseling programs ignored the study of culture in counseling (Ponterotto & Casas, 1987), but, more recently, training programs have begun to include multicultural issues in the curricula (Ponterotto & Casas, 1991). In fact, from 1989 to 1991, multicultural counseling courses were the most frequently added new courses to counseling curricula (Hollis & Wantz, 1990). Concern has been expressed, however, that the outcome and effectiveness of these courses have rarely been evaluated (Ponterotto & Casas, 1991). In response to these concerns, researchers have begun to develop assessment devices that measure a counselor's multicultural counseling competence. In the professional literature, multicultural competence is generally defined as having satisfactory levels of multicultural awareness, knowledge, and skills. Four such instruments discussed in recent counseling literature are the Cross-Cultural Counseling Inventory-Revised (CCCI-R; LaFromboise, Coleman, & Hernandez, 1991), the Multicultural Counseling Awareness Scale—Form B (MCAS:B; Ponterotto, Sanchez, & Magids, 1991), the Multicultural Counseling Inventory (MCI; Sodowsky, Taffe, Gutkin, & Wise, 1992), and the Multicultural Awareness/Knowledge/Skills Survey (MAKSS; D'Andrea, Daniels, & Heck, 1991).

Of the four instruments, only the Cross-Cultural Counseling Inventory-Revised (CCCI-R) is not a self-assessment instrument. The CCCI-R is a 20-item Likert-type instrument completed by a supervisor who has observed a counselor in a cross-cultural dyadic encounter. The instrument is best utilized as a unidimensional assessment, yielding one total score per respondent. The CCCI-R has acceptable levels of internal consistency and moderate levels of construct- and criterion related-validity. The instrument is very brief, making it easy to administer and score.

The Multicultural Counseling Awareness Scale—Form B (MCAS:B) is a 45-item, Likert-type counselor self-assessment. A counselor can complete the instrument in 15 to 20 minutes. The MCAS:B is a bidimensional instrument, yielding two separate subscale scores, one for knowledge/skills and one for awareness. The instrument has acceptable levels of internal consistency as well as construct- and criterion-related validity. Appendix II presents the MCAS:B along with directions for scoring.

The Multicultural Counseling Inventory (MCI) is a 43-item, Likert-type assessment that takes 15 to 20 minutes to complete. The instrument is multidimensional, yielding separate subscale scores for multicultural skills, awareness, knowledge, and the counseling relationship. The MCI has acceptable levels of internal consistency and support for both construct- and criterion-related validity.

Finally, the Multicultural Awareness/Knowledge/Skills Survey (MAKSS) is a 60-item, Likert-type self-assessment. The MAKSS measures three dimensions—awareness, knowledge, and skills—and takes from 20-30 minutes to complete. Although psychometric information is limited at this time, the available research indicates acceptable internal consistency and initial construct- and criterion-related validity. Recently, Ponterotto, Rieger, Barrett, and Sparks (in press) provided a detailed psychometric critique of these four instruments.

Guidelines for Selecting Multicultural Instruments

This chapter has briefly reviewed a number of multicultural-focused instruments. Paper-and-pencil assessments are one tool counselors can use to assist their own professional development and/or to supplement their work with clients and students. These instruments are not panaceas, and they cannot substitute for meaningful personal and professional experience or seasoned clinical judgment.

Any instrument used by counselors should be selected with caution. Below are three general guidelines that we use when selecting instruments for research and practice.

1. Does the instrument have face validity to you? Despite the psychometric properties specified for the instrument, are you comfortable with the scale? Are you satisfied with the wording, format, and length of the instrument? Do you believe it is accurately and clearly measuring its purported construct? Is the wording (e.g., reading level needed for reliable comprehension) appropriate for your target sample? Are there bilingual and/or translation issues that need to be addressed? One rule of thumb is not to administer to clients or students any instrument that you yourself have not completed.
2. Is the instrument reliable and valid from a strict psychometric perspective? Is the scale internally consistent (reliable)? Are indices of validity reported and carefully explained in the written reports on the instrument? Finally, if the instrument claims to be multidimensional, is there empirical and rational support for scoring and interpreting subscales separately? If your familiarity with counseling research and measurement is limited, consult a general counseling research text (e.g., Heppner, Kivlighan, & Wampold, 1992) or multicultural counseling research text (Ponterotto & Casas, 1991).
3. Remember that when requesting an instrument from an author or publisher it is equally important to have all the research reports-to-date on

the instrument. Simply having a copy of the instrument itself will do you little good. It is always a good practice to write to the author of the instrument to request the most recent research and administration/ scoring guidelines. This practice is particularly important if the instrument has not yet been the subject of a thorough, published psychometric critique.

Research Needs in Prejudice Prevention

It is clear that with regard to preventing or reducing prejudice, we have many more questions than answers. As the demography of the United States continues to change rapidly, and as the international community becomes increasing interdependent, the study of interethnic relations will become increasingly important. We close this chapter with two categories of questions needing further research. Although many of the questions have been answered in part throughout this book, there remain many unanswered questions.

Development of Prejudice

Is it possible to eliminate negative ethnic prejudice, or at best should we hope to suppress it and minimize its active expression? How does prejudice develop? What kinds of parental child-rearing practices are conducive to raising prejudice-free children? What about school practices? How do we foster healthy racial/ethnic identity development in children, adolescents, and adults? How strong is the link between a healthy sense of self (e.g., self-esteem, healthy ethnic identity) and prejudice? How do political conditions (e.g., conservative versus liberal Supreme Court or White House) and economic conditions (e.g., recession of the early 1990s) affect the nature, intensity, and expression of prejudice?

Reducing Prejudice

What are the most effective interventions in combating prejudice? What combination of cognitive and affective programming is most conducive to attitude and behavioral change? What are the long-term impacts of various types of prejudice-prevention interventions? Is prejudice-prevention work in the 1990s really a crucial prerequisite to a tolerant and accepting society in the fast-approaching twenty-first century?

Chapter Summary

This chapter has highlighted the importance of assessment, evaluation, and accountability in the area of prejudice prevention. Leading instruments designed to measure racism, discrimination, racial identity, and multicultural counseling awareness and knowledge were reviewed. Guidelines for selecting multicultural instrumentation were presented and directions for needed research were specified. Two measurement instruments are presented in their entirety in Appendix I and II.

11

A Race Awareness Resource Guide
for Counselors and Educators

For counselors and educators to work effectively in the area of prejudice prevention, they must have at their disposal a wide array of resources and referrals. This chapter discusses select resources covering national organizations, books, special journal issues, and films. These resources can assist the counselor in building multicultural understanding, tolerance, and appreciation.

National Organizations

Two major national organizations active in the fight to stem the tide of prejudice and racism are listed below. Keep in mind that there are also many local organizations and committees and divisions within professional organizations that are active in the area. The reader should consult any number of these sources when researching these topics and preparing programs. However, the following organizations serve as an ideal starting point:

The Anti-Defamation League of B'nai B'rith. 823 United Nations Plaza, New York, NY 10017.

> This organization publishes and distributes numerous print and audio-visual material pertaining to these topics.

The National Institute Against Prejudice and Violence. 525 West Redwood Street, Baltimore, MD 21201 [301-528-5170].

This agency acts as a clearinghouse for information on prejudice and racism. It has published numerous reports and monographs that are invaluable to the educator. The institute is also actively involved in research and provides consultation to agencies and communities responding to prejudice.

Professional Books/Monographs

Allport, G. W. (1979). *The nature of prejudice.* Reading, MA: Addison-Wesley.

This 25th anniversary edition of Allport's (1954) seminal text is a must reading for all counselors and educators. Allport provides an in-depth and comprehensive look at prejudice in all its manifestations and developments. The writing is clear, lucid, and filled with interesting and striking examples and anecdotes. Although first published some 40 years ago, the book is still relevant and should be read before more current writing and research.

Barbarin, O. A., Good, P. R., Pharr, O. M., & Siskind, J. A. (Eds.). (1981). *Institutional racism and community competence* (DHHS Publication No. ADM 81-907). Rockville, MD: National Institute of Mental Health. (Contact Center for Minority Group Mental Health Programs, 5600 Fishers Lane, Rockville, MD 20857).

This helpful monograph consists of 22 chapters organized into five sections: theoretical models, cultural diversity, organizational and environmental perspectives, assessment of racism, and interventions. The monograph is more pragmatic than most of the texts listed in this section and has important information on measuring/assessing racism and planning intervention programs on an institution-wide basis.

Bowser, B. P., & Hunt, R. G. (Eds.). (1981). *Impacts of racism on White Americans.* Beverly Hills, CA: Sage.

This enlightening book contains 12 chapters written by leading researchers in the field. The contributions focus on the harmful and debilitating effects of racism on the perpetrators. This is an important contribution because it provides a necessary balance to the majority of the literature that examines the effects of racism on the victims.

Dovidio, J. F., & Gaertner, S. L. (Eds.). (1986). *Prejudice, discrimination, and racism.* Orlando, FL: Academic Press.

This book has 11 chapters written by leading researchers in the area of racism. Topics covered include historical perspectives, forms of racism, understanding stereotyping, racism in the courtroom, and future perspectives.

Essed, P. (1991). *Understanding everyday racism.* Newbury Park, CA: Sage.

> This book presents the results of a comprehensive study of "everyday racism." Essed interviewed African American women in California and Black Surinamese women in the Netherlands. Through her revealing interviews, Essed answers some important questions: "How is racism experienced in everyday situations? How do Blacks recognize covert expressions of racism? What knowledge of racism do Blacks have, and how is this knowledge acquired?" (p. vii).

Katz, P. A., & Taylor, D. A. (Eds.). (1988). *Eliminating racism: Profiles in controversy.* New York: Plenum.

> Similar in format to the Dovidio and Gaertner text (above), this volume presents 19 contributions written by some of the country's leading psychologists specializing in racism. The book provides comprehensive coverage of the topic and covers theoretical controversies, racism toward specific groups (African Americans, Hispanic Americans, Japanese Americans, American Indians, and an enlightening chapter on the interface of racism and sexism), social policy, and affirmative action.

Simpson, G. E., & Yinger, J. M. (1985). *Racial and cultural minorities: An analysis of prejudice and discrimination* (5th ed.). New York: Plenum.

> This classic contribution to the study of minority groups and discrimination is packed with information. The book includes 18 chapters divided into three major parts: causes and consequences of prejudice and discrimination; minorities in the social structure: the institutional patterns of intergroup relations; and prejudice, discrimination, and democratic values.

Troyna, B., & Hatcher, R. (1992). *Racism in children's lives: A study of mainly White primary schools.* London: Routledge.

> This book summarizes the findings of a revealing study of three, primarily White primary schools in Great Britain. To conduct their study, the authors spent a term in each of the three schools. They talked to White and Black pupils individually and in small groups. The result is an enlightening study of how racial issues emerge for and are manifested in young children.

van Dijk, T. A. (1987). *Communicating racism.* Newbury Park, CA: Sage.

> This book reports on the extensive research program of van Dijk at the University of Amsterdam. In *Communicating Racism,* van Dijk analyzes 150 interviews conducted in San Diego, California, and Amsterdam, the Netherlands. A unique and enlightening contribution, this book uncovers how ethnic prejudices are expressed, communicated, and shared within the dominant culture. Unlike the majority of research on racism, which is social psychological in nature, van Dijk's contribution is interdisciplinary, tapping new theoretical developments in cognitive psychology, microsociology, communication, and discourse analysis.

Workbooks

The following books are filled with valuable exercises, programs, and bibliographies. Unlike the professional books, which are well-grounded in theory and research, these books are more pragmatic and are particularly useful for counselors and educators implementing race awareness or prejudice-prevention programs.

Chambers, B., & Pettman, J. (1986). *Anti-racism: A handbook for educators.* Human Rights Commission Education Series No. 1. Canberra, Australia: Australian Government Publishing Service.

This workbook focuses on eradicating racism in Australia, and its contents and usefulness transcend national boundaries. This volume presents an understanding of racism, a rationale for its elimination, strategies for intervention, and an extensive bibliography (books, films, journals).

Hoopes, D. S., & Ventura, P. (1979). *Intercultural sourcebook: Cross-cultural training methodologies.* Chicago, IL: The Society for Intercultural Education, Training and Research. Intercultural Press. (70 W. Hubbard Street, Chicago, IL, 60610)

This valuable sourcebook presents detailed descriptions of exercises and training methods for use in cross-cultural training. Among the training methods described are role-plays, simulations, the Culture Assimilator, self-awareness inventories, critical incidents and case studies.

Katz, J. H. (1978). *White awareness: Handbook for anti-racism training.* Norman, Oklahoma: University of Oklahoma Press.

Katz presents a comprehensive experiential program for anti-racism training for White people. Her White-on-White systematic training program is designed to help White people acknowledge their "Whiteness" and their role in perpetuating a racist status quo. The program helps White people "liberate themselves from the oppressiveness of racism in their lives" (p. vii). The experiential workshop is designed to empower participants to make individual action plans to combat racism in themselves and in society. This book, particularly, serves as a valuable source because its many exercises are well-presented, with clear process guidelines given to the facilitator.

Pasternak, M. G. (1979). *Helping kids learn multi-cultural concepts: A handbook of strategies.* Champaign, IL: Research Press (2612 N. Mattis Avenue, Champaign, IL 61820).

This is an invaluable source for counselors and educators designing multicultural environments and climates in elementary schools. It reports on a comprehensive multicultural implementation program sponsored jointly by an urban school district, three universities, and community personnel (all in Tennessee). The cooperative venture serves as an exemplary role model for other partnership programs. The book itself includes over 100 classroom activities designed to help students appreciate and respect their own and others' ethnic groups and cultures. Also included are components on developing a multicultural resource center and implementing in-service training efforts.

Peters, W. (1987). *A class divided: Then and now.* New Haven, CT: Yale University Press.

This book (the expanded version of Peter's earlier book) summarizes the classic experimental simulation of racism conducted by Jane Elliott, a 3rd grade teacher at the Community Elementary School in Riceville, Iowa. The accompanying films, "The Eye of the Storm" and "A Class Divided" (see related section at the end of this chapter), are among the most valued resources in racism awareness. This book would be helpful to the counselor in preparation for processing the strong reactions to the film or to similar simulations.

Additional Noteworthy Books

Byrnes, D. A. (1987). *Teacher, they called me _____!: Prejudice and discrimination in the classroom.* New York: Anti-Defamation League of B'nai B'rith.

Duckitt, J. (1992). *The social psychology of prejudice.* New York: Praeger.

Feagin, J., & Feagin, D. (1978). *Discrimination American style: Institutional racism and sexism.* Englewood Cliffs, NJ: Prentice Hall.

Gabelko, N. H., & Michaelis, J. L. (1981). *Reducing adolescent prejudice: A handbook.* New York: Teachers College Press, Columbia University.

Guidelines for selecting bias-free textbooks and storybooks. (1981). Council on Interracial Books for Children. Broadway, New York.

Hidalgo, N. M., McDowell, C. L., & Siddle, E. V. (Eds.). (1990). *Facing racism in education (Reprint Series No. 21, Harvard Educational Review).* Cambridge, MA: Harvard College. (Gutman Library Suite 349, 6 Appian Way, Cambridge, MA 02138).

Lynch, E. W., & Hanson, M. J. (1992). *Developing cross-cultural competence: A guide for working with young children and their families.* Baltimore, MD: Paul H. Brooks.

Pettigrew, T. F., Fredrickson, G. M., Knobel, D. T., Glazer, N., & Veda, R. (Eds.) (1982). *Prejudice: Dimensions of ethnicity.* Cambridge, MA: Harvard University Press.

Schniedwind, N., & Davidson, E. (1983). *Open minds to equality.* Englewood Cliffs, NJ: Prentice Hall.

Sedlacek, W., & Brooks, G. (1976). *Racism in American education: A model for change.* Chicago, IL: Nelson Hall.

Shiman, D. A. (1979). *The prejudice book: Activities for the classroom.* New York: The Anti-Defamation League of B'nai B'rith.

Films/Videos

Research has found that films can reduce prejudice (see Pate, 1988). Recommended films are those that are realistic, have a plot, and portray believable characters. It is important that the film audience be able to identify with the emotions, fears, problems, and dreams of the film's characters. There are hundreds of films and videos that can be used in race-appreciation and prejudice-prevention training. Many of the handbooks annotated earlier in this chapter list sample films. Three of the more popular documentary-type films are:

The Eye of the Storm. The 1970 ABC News Documentary. Available from Guidance Associates, The Center for Humanities, Communications Park, Box 3000, Mount Kisco, New York, 10549 (800-431-1242).

A Class Divided. The 1985 Public Broadcasting System Frontline Documentary. Available from PBS Video, 1320 Braddock Place, Alexandria, Virginia, 22314-1698 (800-344-3337).

Names Can Really Hurt Us. A 1988 WCBS-TV film documentary. The Resolving Conflict Creatively Program, New York City Board of Education and Educators for Social Responsibility.

In addition to these and other documentary-type films, counselors and educators may want to show popular films to their groups. For example, Spike Lee's films, *Do the Right Thing, Jungle Fever,* and *Malcolm X* serve as excellent resource films for young and older adults.

Working With Book and Film Resources

In their day-to-day work, counselors and educators often come across material (e.g., newspaper accounts, commission reports, television shows, popular movies, novels) that could be incorporated in multicultural sensitivity training. There are literally hundreds of fiction and nonfiction books and films that can stimulate healthy discussion of racial/ethnic issues. Counselors and educators should work towards developing their own personal library of such resources.

An important point to consider when selecting and incorporating resources for race appreciation interventions is how the material is to be used. During the last 10 years, we have consulted on the topic of prejudice with numerous schools, colleges, agencies, and corporations. We have found that many staff trainers are not clear on how best to utilize stimulus materials. For example, showing the powerful movie *Do the Right Thing* (by Spike Lee) will do little good unless the group facilitator is knowledgeable and comfortable processing reactions to the movie. Here are two guidelines to follow when selecting and preparing resource materials for use in small or large groups:

1. Read and view the material yourself before using it with your group. Therefore, if you incorporate popular novels or films, you should be very familiar with the content and the questions and reactions the material stimulated in you.
2. Prepare stimulus questions for group discussion. Hopefully, the questions will stimulate not just thought but also internal feelings in your participants. Naturally, the conditions for racial identity development and critical thinking reviewed in Chapter 6 (e.g., a climate of trust and safety) are prerequisite to program success. Depending on the developmental group you are working with and the nature of the material, you may want to begin with less (or more) controversial or thought-provoking questions. As the group begins to develop feelings of trust and safety among the members you can then move to more personal questions for discussion.

Below we provide two sets of stimulus questions, one for a documentary and one for a popular movie (both mentioned earlier):

Stimulus Questions for "Eye of the Storm"

We use the following questions in our counselor- and teacher-training programs:

1. What are some of the feelings that emerged for you while viewing the film?
2. Have there been times in your life when you felt like the "blue-eyed" or "brown-eyed" children? Describe these memories.
3. What do you think of Jane Elliott? Cold you see yourself utilizing such a simulation with your class (or group)? Why or why not?
4. Does prejudice-prevention programming need to incorporate "an experience of discrimination"? Can I understand prejudice without having experienced it directly?
5. What are the ethical concerns you see in subjecting children/adolescents/adults to a potentially powerful experience of prejudice? Are the risks worth the

benefits? What precautions can be taken to assure no lasting psychological damage is done to participants?

6. What does the film say about the effects of the teacher's negative expectations on the children's academic performance and classroom behavior? Do you think this has been an issue in the education of children in this country?

Stimulus Questions for "Do The Right Thing"

We have found this movie and the accompanying questions useful in our race relations work with college students, graduate students, and other adults.

1. Which character in the movie can you most identify with and why?
2. What is your personal reaction to the end of the movie?
3. How might the climactic incident of this movie have been avoided?
4. What message is Spike Lee attempting to get across in the movie?
5. Do you believe the riots in Los Angeles, California, in 1992 give some validity to Spike Lee's message? (The movie was produced in 1989.)

Racial Identity Exercise for "Do The Right Thing"

After showing the movie and processing the film (about 4 hours, using one long session or two shorter sessions) we often have our audience match the racial identity stages (Chapters 4 and 5) with the lead characters in the movie. The movie cast is interethnic and we have found it valuable to lead a discussion of each lead character and identify (with rationale) his/her stage of racial identity.

Chapter Summary

This final chapter of *Preventing Prejudice* has abstracted a very selective resource guide for the practicing counselor and educator. We suggested that professionals work toward developing their own resource library on the topic. Important guidelines for selecting, using, and processing resource aids were presented.

Yet the situation is not without its hopeful features. Chief among these is the simple fact that human nature seems, on the whole, to prefer the sight of kindness and friendliness to the sight of cruelty.

(Allport, 1954, p. xiii-xiv).

Appendix I

Social Attitude Survey**

Please respond to all items in the survey. Remember there are no right or wrong answers. The survey is completely anonymous; do not put your name on the survey. Please circle the appropriate number to the right.

	Strongly Disagree	Disagree	Not Sure	Agree	Strongly Agree
1. I do think it is more appropriate for the mother of a newborn baby, rather than the father, to stay home with the baby during the first year.	1	2	3	4	5
2. It is not as easy for women to succeed in business as it is for men.	1	2	3	4	5
3. I really think affirmative action programs on college campuses constitute reverse discrimination.	1	2	3	4	5
4. All Americans should learn to speak two languages.	1	2	3	4	5
5. It upsets (or angers) me that a woman has never been President of the United States.	1	2	3	4	5
6. Generally speaking, men work harder than women.	1	2	3	4	5
7. My friendship network is very racially mixed.	1	2	3	4	5
8. I am against affirmative action programs in business.	1	2	3	4	5
9. I would feel O.K. about my son or daughter dating someone from a different race.	1	2	3	4	5
10. It upsets (or angers) me that a racial minority person has never been President of the United States.	1	2	3	4	5
11. In the past few years there has been too much attention directed toward multicultural or minority issues in education.	1	2	3	4	5
12. I think feminist perspectives should be an integral part of the higher education curriculum.	1	2	3	4	5
13. Most of my close friends are from my own racial group.	1	2	3	4	5

14. I feel somewhat more secure that a man rather than a woman is currently President of the United States.   1   2   3   4   5

15. In the past few years there has been too much attention directed towards multicultural or minority issues in business.   1   2   3   4   5

16. Overall, I think racial minorities in America complain too much about racial discrimination.   1   2   3   4   5

17. I think the President of the United States should make a concerted effort to appoint more women and racial minorities to the country's Supreme Court.   1   2   3   4   5

18. I think white people's racism toward racial minority groups still constitutes a major problem in America.   1   2   3   4   5

19. I think the school system, from elementary school through college, should encourage minority and immigrant children to learn and fully adopt traditional American values.   1   2   3   4   5

20. I think there is as much female violence towards men as there is male violence toward women.   1   2   3   4   5

21. I think the school system, from elementary school through college, should promote traditional American values as well as the values representative of the culturally diverse students in the class.   1   2   3   4   5

22. I believe that reading the autobiography of Malcolm X would be of value.   1   2   3   4   5

23. I would enjoy living in a neighborhood consisting of a racially diverse population (i.e., Asians, Blacks, Hispanics, Whites).   1   2   3   4   5

24. I think it is better if people marry within their own race.   1   2   3   4   5

25. Women make too big of a deal out of sexual harassment issues in the workplace.   1   2   3   4   5

NOTE: **The actual name of this instrument is the *Quick Discrimination Index*. Copyright © 1992 by Joseph G. Ponterotto and Alan Burkard

157

Quick Discrimination Index (QDI)

Scoring Directions

Note that on the instrument itself, the title "Quick Discrimination Index" does not appear; instead, the title "Social Attitude Survey" appears in an attempt to avoid initial respondent reactivity.

The QDI consists of 25 items and reports a single total score that represents the respondent's level of awareness, knowledge, and sensitivity to racial/ethnic minority issues and women's issues. Pilot research on the QDI shows the instrument to be internally consistent (Coefficient Alpha of .89) and valid.

Of the 25 items on the QDI, 11 are worded and scored in a positive direction (high scores indicate high sensitivity to multicultural issues), and 14 are worded and scored in a negative direction (where low scores are indicative of sensitivity). Naturally, when tallying the Total Score response, these 14 items need to be *reverse-scored*.

For the following eleven QDI items simply list the actual number circled and add across:

4____, 5____, 7____, 9____, 10____, 12____,
17____, 18____, 21____, 22____, 23____   Subtotal____

For the following fourteen QDI items reverse the score of each circled item as follows:

Score of 1 = 5

Score of 2 = 4

Score of 3 = 3

Score of 4 = 2

Score of 5 = 1

(For example if you circled number 4 for item one, then put a 2 in the first space below.)

1____, 2____, 3____, 6____, 8____, 11____, 13____, 14____,
15____, 16____, 19____, 20____, 24____, 25____

                                        Subtotal____

For the total score simply add the two subtotal scores.

Subtotal score____ + Subtotal score____ = TOTAL SCORE____

Although interpretation guidelines for the scoring are currently being researched, pilot research indicates that the mean score for a heterogeneous sample is 85. The score range is from 25 to 125. General guidelines are as follows:

- Score of 25-50 indicates the respondent is very insensitive to and unaware of minority and women's issues.

- Score of 51-75 indicates low sensitivity and little awareness of minority and women's issues.

- Score of 76-100 indicates moderate sensitivity to and knowledge of minority and women's issues.

- Score of 101-125 indicates high sensitivity to and knowledge of minority and women's issues.

These scoring ranges are very broad, and the instrument at this time should not be used as a diagnostic or assessment tool. The reader should refer to Ponterotto et al (1993) for more detailed information on the Quick Discrimination Index.

Appendix II

Multicultural Counseling Awareness Scale (MCAS)

Form B: Revised Self-Assessment

Using the following scale, rate the truth of each item as it applies to you.

1	2	3	4	5	6	7
not at all true			*somewhat true*			*totally true*

1. I am familiar with the research and writings of Janet E. Helms and I can discuss her work at length spontaneously.

   1   2   3   4   5   6   7

2. I believe all clients should maintain direct eye contact during counseling.

   1   2   3   4   5   6   7

3. I check up on my minority/cultural counseling skills by monitoring my functioning—via consultation, supervision, and continual education.

   1   2   3   4   5   6   7

4. I am familiar with the research and writings of Derald Wing Sue and I can discuss his work at length spontaneously.

   1   2   3   4   5   6   7

5. I am aware some research indicates that minority clients receive "less preferred" forms of counseling treatment than majority clients.

   1   2   3   4   5   6   7

6. I think that clients who do not discuss intimate aspects of their lives are being resistant and defensive.

   1   2   3   4   5   6   7

7. I am aware of certain counseling skills, techniques, or approaches that are more likely to transcend culture and be effective with any clients.

   1   2   3   4   5   6   7

8. I am aware that the use of standard English with a lower-income or bilingual client may result in misperceptions of the client's strengths and weaknesses.

   1   2   3   4   5   6   7

9. I am familiar with the "culturally deficient" and "culturally deprived" depiction of minority mental health and understand how these labels serve to foster and perpetuate discrimination.

   1   2   3   4   5   6   7

10. I am familiar with the research and writings of Donald R. Atkinson and I can discuss his work at length spontaneously.

    1   2   3   4   5   6   7

11. I feel all the recent attention directed toward multicultural issues in counseling is overdone and not really warranted.

    1   2   3   4   5   6   7

1	2	3	4	5	6	7
not at all true			*somewhat true*			*totally true*

12. I am aware of the individual differences that exist within members of a particular ethnic group based on values and beliefs, and level of acculturation.

   1   2   3   4   5   6   7

13. I am aware some research indicates that minority clients are more likely to be diagnosed with mental illnesses than are majority clients.

   1   2   3   4   5   6   7

14. I think that clients should perceive the nuclear family as the ideal social unit.

   1   2   3   4   5   6   7

15. I believe that being highly competitive and achievement oriented are traits that all clients should work towards.

   1   2   3   4   5   6   7

16. I am familiar with the research and writings of J. Manuel Casas and I can discuss his work at length spontaneously.

   1   2   3   4   5   6   7

17. I am aware of my limitations in cross-cultural counseling and could specify them readily.

   1   2   3   4   5   6   7

18. I am familiar with the research and writings of Paul B. Pedersen and I can discuss his work at length spontaneously.

   1   2   3   4   5   6   7

19. I am aware of the differential effects of nonverbal communication (e.g. personal space, eye contact, handshakes) on different ethnic cultures.

   1   2   3   4   5   6   7

20. I understand the impact and operations of oppression and the racist concepts that have permeated the mental health professions.

   1   2   3   4   5   6   7

21. I realize that counselor-client incongruities in problem conceptualization and counseling goals often reduce counselor credibility.

   1   2   3   4   5   6   7

22. I am familiar with the research and writings of Michael Santana-DeVio and I can discuss his work at length spontaneously.

   1   2   3   4   5   6   7

23. I am aware that some minorities see psychology functioning to maintain and promote the status and power of the White Establishment.

   1   2   3   4   5   6   7

24. I am knowledgeable of acculturation models for various ethnic minority groups.

   1   2   3   4   5   6   7

25. I have an understanding of the role culture and racism play in the development of identity and world views among minority groups.

   1   2   3   4   5   6   7

1	2	*3*	*4*	5	6	*7*
not at all true			*somewhat true*			*totally true*

26. I believe that it is important to emphasize objective and rational thinking in minority clients.

     1   2   3   4   5   6   7

27. I am aware of culture-specific, that is culturally indigenous, models of counseling for various racial/ethnic groups.

     1   2   3   4   5   6   7

28. I believe that my clients should view a patriarchal structure as the ideal.

     1   2   3   4   5   6   7

29. I am aware of both the barriers and benefits related to cross-cultural counseling.

     1   2   3   4   5   6   7

30. At this point in my professional development, I feel very competent counseling the culturally different.

     1   2   3   4   5   6   7

31. I am comfortable with differences that exist between me and my clients in terms of race and beliefs.

     1   2   3   4   5   6   7

32. I am aware of institutional barriers that may inhibit minorities from using mental health services.

     1   2   3   4   5   6   7

33. I am aware that counselors frequently impose their own cultural values upon minority clients.

     1   2   3   4   5   6   7

34. I think that my clients should exhibit some degree of psychological mindedness and sophistication .

     1   2   3   4   5   6   7

35. I am familiar with the research and writings of Teresa D. LaFromboise and I can discuss her work at length spontaneously.

     1   2   3   4   5   6   7

36. I believe that minority clients will benefit most from counseling with a majority counselor who endorses White middle class values and norms.

     1   2   3   4   5   6   7

37. I am aware that being born a White person in this society carries with it certain advantages.

     1   2   3   4   5   6   7

38. At this point in my professional development, I feel I could benefit little from clinical supervision of my multicultural client caseload.

     1   2   3   4   5   6   7

1	2	3	4	5	6	7
not at all true			*somewhat true*			*totally true*

39. I feel that different socioeconomic status backgrounds of counselor and client may serve as an initial barrier to effective cross-cultural counseling.

    1   2   3   4   5   6   7

40. I have a clear understanding of the value assumptions inherent in the major schools of counseling and know how these interact with values of the culturally diverse.

    1   2   3   4   5   6   7

41. I am aware that some minorities see the counseling process as contrary to their own life experiences and inappropriate or insufficient to their needs.

    1   2   3   4   5   6   7

42. I am aware that being born a minority in this society brings with it certain challenges that White people do not have to face.

    1   2   3   4   5   6   7

43. I believe that all clients must view themselves as their number-one responsibility.

    1   2   3   4   5   6   7

44. I am sensitive to circumstances (personal biases, stage of ethnic identity) which may dictate referral of the minority client to a member of his/her own race/culture.

    1   2   3   4   5   6   7

45. I am aware that some minorities believe counselors lead minority students into nonacademic programs regardless of student potential, preferences, or ambitions.

    1   2   3   4   5   6   7

Thank you for completing this scale, and feel free to express below any comments, concerns, or questions you have about this instrument.

_____
_____
_____

Scoring Directions (As of February, 1991)

Knowledge Scale = 1, 3, 4, 5, 7, 9, 10, 12, 13, 16, 17, 18, 19, 20, 21, 23, 24, 25, 27, 29, 31, 32, 33, 35, 40, 41, 44, 45.
   Score Range = 28 to 196; Higher scores signify greater multicultural knowledge/skills.
Awareness Scale = (2), (6), 8, (11), (14), (15), (26), (28), (34), (36), 37, 39, 42, (43).
   Note: Items in parentheses are to be reverse scored.
   Score Range = 14 to 98; Higher scores indicate greater multicultural awareness.
Total Scale Score = 42 to 294 (Note: three items below *are not* included in scale scores.)
   Social Desirability Items = 22, 30, 38
   Score Range = 3 to 21; Higher scores indicate tendency to want to "look good" on scale results. Research is currently under way to determine the social desirability cutoff score. At this time, any score above 15 is considered indicative of social desirability contamination.

SOURCE: Copyright by Joseph G. Ponterotto, Caridad M. Sanchez, and Debbie M. Magids, Fordham University at Lincoln Center, Graduate School of Education

References

Aboud, F. E. (1987). The development of ethnic self-identification and attitudes. In J. S. Phinney & M. J. Rotheram (Eds.), *Children's ethnic socialization: Pluralism and development* (pp. 32-55). Newbury Park, CA: Sage.

Albee, G. W., Bond, L. A., & Monsey, T.B.C. (Eds.). (1992). *Improving children's lives: Global Perspectives on prevention.* Newbury Park, CA: Sage.

Alexander, C. M. (1992). *Construct validity and reliability of the White Racial Identity Attitude Scale.* Unpublished doctoral dissertation, University of Nebraska–Lincoln.

Allport, G. W. (1954). *The nature of prejudice.* Reading, MA: Addison-Wesley.

Allport, G. W. (1979). *The nature of prejudice* (25th anniversary ed.). Reading, MA: Addison-Wesley.

Altbach, P. (1991). The racial dilemma in American higher education. In P. G. Altbach & K. Lomotey (Eds.), *The racial crisis in American higher education* (pp. 3-19). Albany, NY: State University of New York Press.

Arce, C. A. (1981). A reconsideration of Chicano culture and identity. *Daedalus, 110,* 177-192.

Atkinson, D. R., & Hackett, G. (Eds.). (1988). *Counseling non-ethnic American minorities.* Springfield, IL: Charles C Thomas.

Atkinson, D. R., Morten, G., & Sue, D. W. (Eds.). (1989). *Counseling American minorities: A cross-cultural perspective* (3rd ed.). Dubuque, Iowa: William C. Brown.

Atkinson, D. R., Morten, G., & Sue, D. W. (Eds.). (1993). *Counseling American minorities: A cross-cultural perspective* (4th ed.). Dubuque, Iowa: William C. Brown.

Atkinson, D. R., Thompson, C. E., & Grant, S. K. (1993). A three-dimensional model for counseling racial/ethnic minorities. *The Counseling Psychologist, 21,* 257-277.

Axelson, J. A. (1985). *Counseling and development in a multicultural society.* Monterey, CA: Brooks/Cole.

Balanger, V. J., Hoffman, M. A., & Sedlacek, W. E. (1992). Racial attitudes among incoming White students: A study of 10-year trends. *Journal of College Student Development, 33,* 245-252.

Baldwin, J. A., & Bell, Y. R. (1985). The African Self-Consciousness scale: An Africentric personality questionnaire. *The Western Journal of Black Studies, 9,* 61-68.

Barbarin, O. A., & Gilbert, R. (1981). Institutional racism scale: Assessing self and organizational attributes. In O. A. Barbarin, P. R. Good, O. M. Pharr, & J. A. Siskind (Eds.), *Institutional racism and community competence* (DHSS Publication No. ADM 81-907, pp. 147-171). Rockville, MD: National Institute of Mental Health, Center for Minority Group Mental Health Programs.

Barbarin, O. A., Good, P. R., Pharr, O. M., & Siskind, J. A. (Eds.). (1981). *Institutional racism and community competence* (DHSS Publication No. ADM 81-907). Rockville, MD: National Institute of Mental Health, Center for Minority Group Mental Health Programs.

Belenky, M. F., Clinchy, B. M., Goldberger, N. R., & Tarule, J. M. (1986). *Women's ways of knowing.* New York: Basic Books.

Berry, J. W., & Kim, U. (1988). Acculturation and mental health. In P. R. Dasen, J. W. Berry, & N. Sartorius (Eds.), *Health and cross-cultural psychology: Toward applications* (pp. 207-236). Newbury Park, CA: Sage.

Block, J. H. (1973). Conceptions of sex role: Some cross-cultural and longitudinal perspectives. *American Psychologist, 28,* 512-526.

Boucher, J., Landis, D., & Clark, K. A. (Eds.). (1987). *Ethnic conflict: International perspectives.* Newbury Park, CA: Sage.

Boyle, S. P. (1962). *The desegregated heart.* New York: William Morrow.

Bowser, B. P., & Hunt, R. G. (1981). *Impacts of racism on White Americans.* Beverly Hills, CA: Sage.

Braden, A. (1958). *The wall between.* New York: Monthly Review Press.

Brewer, M., & Miller, N. (1984). Beyond the contact hypothesis: Theoretical perspectives on desegregation. In N. Miller & M. Brewer (Eds.), *Groups in contact: The psychology of desegregation* (pp. 281-302). New York: Academic Press.

Brown, R. D. (1990). Affirmative action and professional associations: Useful strategies. In J. G. Ponterotto, D. E. Lewis, & R. Bullington (Eds.), *Affirmative action on campus* (pp. 75-81). San Francisco, CA: Jossey-Bass.

Byrnes, D. A. (1988). Children and prejudice. *Social Education, 52,* 267-271.

Byrnes, D. A. (1987). *Teacher, they called me a _____!: Prejudice and discrimination in the classroom.* New York: Anti-Defamation League of B'nai B'rith.

Carter, R. T. (1990). The relationship between racism and racial identity among White Americans: An exploratory investigation. *Journal of Counseling and Development, 69,* 46-50.

Carter, R. T. (1991). Racial identity attitudes and psychological functioning. *Journal of Multicultural Counseling and Development, 19,* 105-114.

Carter, R. T., & Helms, J. E. (1990). White racial identity attitudes and cultural values. In J. E. Helms (Ed.), *Black and white racial identity: Theory, research, and practice* (pp. 105-118). New York: Greenwood Press.

Casas, J. M. (1984). Policy, training, and research in counseling psychology: The racial/ethnic minority perspective. In S. D. Brown & R. Lent (Eds.), *Handbook of Counseling Psychology* (pp. 785-831). New York: John Wiley.

Casas, J. M. (1990). Investing in affirmative action: Everyone's responsibility. In J. G. Ponterotto, D. E. Lewis, & R. Bullington (Eds.), *Affirmative action on campus* (pp. 83-88). San Francisco, CA: Jossey-Bass.

Casas, J. M., & Furlong, M. J. (in press). School counselors as advocates for increased Hispanic parent participation in schools. In P. B. Pedersen & J. Carey (Eds.), *Multicultural counseling in schools.* Boston: Allyn & Bacon.

Chambers, B., & Pettman, J. (1986). *Anti-racism: A handbook for adult educators* (Human Rights Commission Education Series No. 1). Canberra, Australia: Australian Government Publishing Service.

Cheatham, H. E. (1991). Affirming affirmative action. In H. E. Cheatham (Ed.), *Cultural pluralism on campus* (pp. 9-23). Alexandria, VA: American College Personnel Association.

Claney, D., & Parker, W. M. (1989). Assessing White racial consciousness and perceived comfort with Black individuals: A preliminary study. *Journal of Counseling and Development, 67,* 449-451.

Clark, K. B. (1955). *Prejudice and your child.* Boston: Beacon Press.

Coyne, R. K. (1987). *Primary preventive counseling: Empowering people and systems.* Muncie, Indiana: Accelerated Development, Inc.

Cross, W. E. (1971). The Negro-to-Black conversion experience: Toward a psychology of Black liberation. *Black World, 20,* 13-27.

Cross, W. E. (1978). The Cross and Thomas models of psychological nigrescence. *Journal of Black Psychology, 5,* 13-19.

Cross, W. E. (1987). A two-factor theory of black identity: Implications for the study of identity development in minority children. In J. S. Phinney & M. J. Rotheram (Eds.), *Children's ethnic socialization: Pluralism and development* (pp. 117-133). Newbury Park, CA: Sage.

Cross, W. E. (1989). Nigrescence: A nondiaphanous phenomena. *The Counseling Psychologist, 17,* 273-276.

Cross, W. E. (1991). *Shades of black: Diversity in African-American Identity.* Philadelphia: Temple University Press.

Cross, W. E., Parham, T. A., & Helms, J. E. (in press). Nigrescence revisited: Theory and research. In R. L. Jones (Ed.), *Advances in black psychology.* Los Angeles: Cobb & Henry.

D'Andrea, M. (1992, October). The violence of our silence: Some thoughts about racism, counseling and development. *Guidepost, 35* (4), 31.

D'Andrea, M., Daniels, J., & Heck, R. (1991). Evaluating the impact of multicultural counseling training. *Journal of Counseling and Development, 70,* 143-150.

D'Angelo, E. (1971). *The teaching of critical thinking.* Amsterdam: B. R. Gruner.

d'Ardenne, P., & Mahtani, A. (1990). *Transcultural counseling in action.* London: Sage.

Dashfsky, A. (Ed.). (1976). *Ethnic identity in society.* Chicago: Rand McNally.

Delworth, U. (1989). Identity in the college years: Issues of gender and ethnicity. *Journal of the National Association of Student Personnel Administrators, 26,* 162-166.

Dennis, R. M. (1981). Socialization and racism: The white experience. In B. P. Bowser & R. G. Hunt (Eds.), *Impacts of racism on white Americans* (pp. 71-85). Beverly Hills, CA: Sage.

Dollard, J. (1937). *Caste and class in a southern town.* New Haven, CT: Yale University Press.

Dovidio, J. F., & Gaertner, S. L. (Eds.) (1986a). *Prejudice, discrimination, and racism.* Orlando, FL: Academic Press.

Dovidio, J. F., & Gaertner, S. L. (1986b). Prejudice, discrimination, and racism: Historical trends and contemporary approaches. In J. F. Dovidio & S. L. Gaertner (Eds.), *Prejudice, discrimination, and racism* (pp. 1-34). Orlando, FL: Academic Press.

D'Souza, D. (1991). *Illiberal education: The politics of race and sex on campus.* New York: Free Press.

Duckitt, J. (1992a). Psychology and prejudice: A historical analysis and integrative framework. *American Psychologist, 47,* 1182-1193.

Duckitt, J. (1992b). *The social psychology of prejudice.* New York: Praeger.

Edler, J. M. (1974). *White on white: An anti-racism manual for white educators in the process of becoming.* Unpublished doctoral dissertation, University of Massachusetts, Amherst.

Ehrlich, H. J. (1990). *Campus ethnoviolence and the policy options.* Institute Report No. 4. Baltimore, MD: National Institute Against Prejudice and Violence.

Erikson, E. H. (1950). *Childhood and society.* New York: Norton.

Erikson, E. H. (1968). *Identity: Youth and crisis.* New York: Norton.

Essed, P. (1991). *Understanding everyday racism: An interdisciplinary theory.* Newbury Park, CA: Sage.

Evans, N. J., & Ochs, N. G. (1991, August). *The effects of multicultural training on white trainees.* Paper presented at the annual meeting of the American Psychological Association, San Francisco, CA.

Farb, P. (1978). *Humankind.* Boston: Houghton Mifflin.

Feagin, J., & Feagin, D. (1978). *Discrimination American style: Institutional Racism and Sexism.* Englewood Cliffs, NJ: Prentice Hall.

Felner, R. D., Jason, L. A., Moritsugu, J. N., & Faber, S. S. (Eds.). (1983). *Preventive psychology: Theory, research and practice.* New York: Pergamon.

Festinger, L. (1954). A theory of social comparison processes. *Human Relations, 7,* 117-140.

Filla, T., & Clark, D. (1973). *Human relations resource guide on in-service programs.* St. Paul, MN: Minnesota Department of Education.

Gabelko, N. H. (1988). Prejudice reduction in secondary schools. *Social Education, 52,* 276-279.

Gabelko, N. H., & Michaelis, J. L. (1981). *Reducing adolescent prejudice: A handbook.* New York: Teachers College Press, Columbia University.

Gaertner, S. L., & Dovidio, J. F. (1986). The aversive form of racism. In J. F. Dovidio & S. L. Gaertener (Eds.), *Prejudice, discrimination, and racism* (pp. 61-89). Orlando, FL: Academic Press.

Gelso, C. J., & Fretz, B. E. (1992). *Counseling psychology.* Fort Worth, Texas: Harcourt Brace Jovanovich.

Gibbs, J. (1988). *Young, black, and male in America: An endangered species.* Dover, MA: Auburn House.

Gilligan, C. (1982). *In a different voice.* Cambridge, MA: Harvard University Press.

Greeley, A. M., & Sheatsley, P. B. (1971). Attitudes toward racial integration. *Scientific American, 225*(6), 13-19.

Green, M. F. (1989). *Minorities on campus: A handbook for enhancing diversity.* Washington, DC: American Council on Education.

Gregory, S. (1970). *Hey, white girl.* New York: W. W. Norton.

Guidelines for selecting bias-free textbooks and storybooks. (1981). New York: Council on Interracial Books for Children.

Halsey, M. (1946). *Color blind.* New York: Simon & Schuster.

Hardiman, R. (1982). *White identity development: A process oriented model for describing the racial consciousness of white Americans.* Unpublished doctoral dissertation, University of Massachusetts, Amherst.

Hayes-Bautista, D. E. (1974). *Becoming Chicano: A dis-assimilation theory of transformation of ethnic identity.* Unpublished doctoral dissertation, University of California, Santa Barbara.

Helms, J. E. (1984). Toward a theoretical model of the effects of race on counseling: A black and white model. *The Counseling Psychologist, 12,* 153-165.

Helms, J. E. (1989). Considering some methodological issues in racial identity counseling research. *The Counseling Psychologist, 17,* 227-252.

Helms, J. E. (1990a). An overview of black racial identity theory. In J. E. Helms (Ed.), *Black and white racial identity: Theory, research, and practice* (pp. 9-32). New York: Greenwood Press.

Helms, J. E. (Ed.). (1990b). *Black and white racial identity: Theory, research, and practice.* New York: Greenwood Press.

Helms, J. E. (1990c). The measurement of black racial identity attitudes. In J. E. Helms (Ed.), *Black and white racial identity: Theory, research, and practice* (pp. 33-47). New York: Greenwood Press.

Helms, J. E. (1990d). Toward a model of white racial identity development. In J. E. Helms (Ed.), *Black and white racial identity: Theory, research, and practice* (pp. 49-66). New York: Greenwood Press.

Helms, J. E. (1992). *A race is a nice thing to have.* Topeka, Kansas: Content Communications.

Helms, J. E. (in press). Racial identity in the school environment. In P. B. Pedersen & J. Carey (Eds.), *Multicultural counseling in schools.* Boston: Allyn & Bacon.

Helms, J. E., & Carter, R. T. (1990a). Development of the White Racial Identity Inventory. In J. E. Helms (Ed.), *Black and white racial identity: Theory, research, and practice* (pp. 67-80). New York: Greenwood Press.

Helms, J. E., & Carter, R. T. (1990b). White racial identity attitude scale (Form WRIAS). In J. E. Helms (Ed.), *Black and white theory, research, and practice* (pp. 249-251). New York: Greenwood Press.

Helms, J. E., & Parham, T. A. (1990). Black Racial Identity Attitude Scale (Form RIAS:B). In J. E. Helms (Ed.), *Black and white racial identity: Theory, research, and practice* (pp. 245-247). New York: Greenwood Press.

Heppner, P. P., Kivlighan, D. M., Jr., & Wampold, B. E. (1992). *Research design in counseling.* Pacific Grove, CA: Brooks/Cole.

Hermalin, J., & Morell, J. A. (Eds.). (1987). *Prevention planning in mental health.* Newbury Park, CA: Sage.

Hess, R. E., & DeLeon, J. (Eds.). (1989). *The National Mental Health Association: Eighty years of involvement in the field of prevention.* New York: Haworth.

Hidalgo, N. M., McDowell, C. L., & Siddle, E. V. (Eds.). (1990). *Facing racism in education* (Reprint Series No. 21). Cambridge, MA: Harvard Educational Review.

Hines, A., & Pedersen, P. (1980). The cultural grid: Matching social system variables and cultural perspectives. *Asian Pacific Training Development Journal, 1* (1), 5-11.

Hollis, J. W., & Wantz, R. A. (1990). *Counselor preparation, 1990-1992: Programs, personnel, trends* (7th ed.). Muncie, IN: Accelerated Development.

Hoopes, D. S., & Ventura, P. (1979). *Intercultural sourcebook: Cross-cultural training methodologies.* Washington, DC: Intercultural Press.

Jackson, B. W. (1976). *The function of a theory of black identity development in achieving relevance in education for black students.* Unpublished doctoral dissertation, University of Massachusetts, Amherst.

Jacobson, C. K. (1985). Resistance to affirmative action: Self-interest or racism. *Journal of Conflict Resolution, 29,* 306-329.

James, C. E. (1990, June). *Career equity for youth: Career development resources and strategies for working with youth of various racial, ethnic and cultural backgrounds.* Paper presented to the Canadian Guidance and Counseling Foundation, Ottawa, Canada.

Jones, J. M. (1972). *Prejudice and racism.* Reading, MA: Addison Wesley.

Jones, J. M. (1981). The concept of racism and its changing reality. In B. J. Bowser & R. G. Hunt (Eds.), *Impacts of racism on white Americans* (pp. 27-49). Beverly Hills, CA: Sage.

Jones, J. M. (1986). Racism: A cultural analysis of the problem. In J. F. Dovidio & S. L. Gaertner (Eds.), *Prejudice, discrimination, and racism* (pp. 279-314). Orlando, FL: Academic Press.

Jones, J. M. (1988). Racism in black and white: A bicultural model of reaction and evolution. In P. A. Katz & D. A. Taylor (Eds.), *Eliminating racism: Profiles in controversy* (pp. 117-135). New York: Plenum.

Josselson, R. (1987). *Finding herself.* San Francisco: Jossey-Bass.

Karp, J. B. (1981). The emotional impact and a model for changing racist attitudes. In B. P. Bowser & R. G. Hunt (Eds.), *Impacts of racism on white Americans* (pp. 87-96). Beverly Hills, CA: Sage.

Katz, J. H. (1978). *White awareness: Handbook for anti-racism training.* Norman, OK: University of Oklahoma Press.

Katz, J. H. (1985). The sociopolitical nature of counseling. *The Counseling Psychologist, 13,* 615-624.

Katz, P. A. (1987). Development and social processes in ethnic attitudes and self-identification. In J. S. Phinney & M. J. Rotheram (Eds.), *Children's ethnic socialization: Pluralism and development* (pp. 92-99). Newbury Park, CA: Sage.

Katz, P. A., & Taylor, D. A. (Eds.) (1988). *Eliminating racism: Profiles in controversy.* New York: Plenum.

Kessler, M., Goldston, S. E., & Joffe, J. M. (Eds.). (1992). *The present and future of prevention.* Newbury Park, CA: Sage.

Kim, J. (1981). *Process of Asian-American identity development: A study of Japanese American women's perceptions of their struggle to achieve positive identities.* Unpublished doctoral dissertation, University of Massachusetts, Amherst.

King, L. (1971). *Confessions of a white racist.* New York: Viking.

Kinzer, S. (1992, September 6). A mayor in Germany acts to prevent attacks on foreigners in eastern city. *The New York Times,* p. L 10.

Kleinman, A. (1980). *Patients and healers in the context of culture.* Berkeley, CA: University of California Press.

Kovel, J. (1970). *White racism: A psychohistory.* New York: Pantheon.

Krogman, W. M. (1945). The concept of race. In R. Linton (Ed.), *The science of man in world crisis* (pp. 38-61). New York: Columbia University Press.

LaFromboise, T. D., Coleman, H.L.K., & Hernandez, A. (1991). Development and factor structure of the Cross-Cultural Counseling Inventory–Revised. *Professional Psychology: Research and Practice, 22,* 380-388.

Landis, D., & Boucher, J. (1987). Themes and models of conflict. In J. Boucher, D. Landis, & K. A. Clark (Eds.), *Ethnic conflict: International perspectives* (pp. 18-32). Newbury Park, CA: Sage.

Lane, P. S., & McWhirter, J. J. (1992). A peer mediation model: Conflict resolution for elementary and middle school children. *Elementary School Guidance and Counseling, 27,* 15-23.

Linton, R. (Ed.). (1945). *The science of man in world crisis.* New York: Columbia University Press.

Lorion, R. P. (Ed.). (1990). *Protecting the children: Strategies for optimizing emotional and behavioral development.* New York: Haworth.

Lynch, E. W., & Hanson, M. J. (1992). *Developing cross-cultural competence: A guide for working with young children and their families*. Baltimore, MD: Paul Brooks.

Marcia, J. (1966). Development and validation of ego-identity status. *Journal of Personality and Social Psychology, 3,* 551-558.

Marcia, J. E. (1980). Identity in adolescence. In J. Adelson (Ed.), *Handbook of adolescent psychology* (pp. 159-187). New York: John Wiley.

McConahay, J. B. (1982). Self-interest versus racial attitudes as correlates of antibusing attitudes in Louisville: Is it the buses or is it the blacks? *Journal of Politics, 44,* 692-720.

McConahay, J. B. (1983). Modern racism and modern discrimination: The effects of race, racial attitudes, and context on simulated hiring decisions. *Personality and Social Psychology Bulletin, 9,* 551-558.

McConahay, J. B. (1986). Modern racism, ambivalence, and the Modern Racism Scale. In J. F. Dovidio & S. L. Gaertner (Eds.), *Prejudice, discrimination, and racism* (pp. 91-125). New York: Academic Press.

McConahay, J. B., & Hough, J. C. (1976). Symbolic racism. *Journal of Social Issues, 32,* 23-45.

McCormick, T. E. (1990). Counselor-teacher interface: Promoting nonsexist education and career development. *Journal of Multicultural Counseling and Development, 18,* 2-10.

McFarland, W. P. (1992). Counselors teaching peaceful conflict resolution. *Journal of Counseling and Development, 71,* 18-21.

Miles, R. (1989). *Racism.* London: Routledge.

Miller, J. B. (1976). *Towards a new psychology of women.* Boston: Beacon Press.

Milliones, J. (1980). Construction of a black consciousness measure: Psychotherapeutic implications. *Psychotherapy: Theory, Research, and Practice, 17,* 175-182.

Mitchell, S. L., & Dell, D. M. (1992). The relationship between black students' racial identity attitude and participation in campus organizations. *Journal of College Student Development, 33,* 39-43.

Mydans, S. (1992, April 30). Los Angeles policemen acquitted in taped beating. *The New York Times,* pp. Al, D22.

Mydans, S., & Marriott, M. (1992, May 18). Riots ruin a business, and a neighborhood suffers. *The New York Times,* pp. Al, B8.

Nottingham, C. R., Rosen, D. H., & Parks, C. (1992). Psychological well-being among African American university students. *Journal of College Student Development, 33,* 356-362.

Parham, T. A. (1989). Cycles of psychological nigrescence. *The Counseling Psychologist, 17,* 187-226.

Parham, T. A., & Helms, J. E. (1981). The influence of black students' racial identity attitudes on preferences for counselor's race. *Journal of Counseling Psychology, 28,* 250-257.

Parham, T. A., & Helms, J. E. (1985a). Attitudes of racial identity and self-esteem of black students: An exploratory investigation. *Journal of College Student Personnel, 26,* 143-147.

Parham, T. A., & Helms, J. E. (1985b). Relation of racial identity attitudes to self-actualization and affective states of black students. *Journal of Counseling Psychology, 32,* 431-440.

Pasternak, M. G. (1979). *Helping kids learn multi-cultural concepts: A handbook of strategies.* Champaign, IL: Research Press.

Pate, G. S. (1988). Research on reducing prejudice. *Social Education, 52,* 287-289.

Pedersen, A., & Pedersen, P. (1989). The cultural grid: A complicated and dynamic approach to multicultural counseling. *Counseling Psychology Quarterly, 2* (2), 133-141.

Pedersen, P. B. (1988). *A handbook for developing multicultural awareness.* Alexandria, VA: American Counseling Association.

Pedersen, P. B. (1991). Multiculturalism as a generic approach to counseling. *Journal of Counseling and Development, 70,* 6-12.

Pedersen, P. B. (1992). *The culture-bound counselor as an unintentional racist.* Manuscript submitted for publication.

Pedersen, P. B. (in press). Multicultural training in schools. In P. B. Pedersen & J. Carey (Eds.), *Multicultural counseling in schools.* Needham, MA: Allyn & Bacon.

Pedersen, P., & Pedersen, A. (1989). The cultural grid: A framework for multicultural counseling. *International Journal for the Advancement of Counseling, 12* (4), 299-307.

Peters, W. (1987). *A class divided: Then and now* (expanded edition). New Haven, CT: Yale University Press.

Peterson, D. P. (1990a). Working against prejudice in a large state university. In G. Stricker, E. Davis-Russell, E. Bourg, E. Duran, W. R. Hammond, J. McHolland, K. Polite, & B. E. Vaughn (Eds.), *Toward ethnic diversification in psychology education and training* (pp. 43-55). Washington, DC: American Psychological Association.

Peterson, D. P. (1990b). *Students speak on prejudice: A survey of intergroup attitudes and ethnoviolent behavior among undergraduate students at Rutgers University.* New Brunswick, NJ: Rutgers University, the State University of New Jersey.

Pettigrew, T. F. (1981). The mental health impact. In B. P. Bowser & R. G. Hunt (Eds.), *Impacts of racism on white Americans.* (pp. 97-118). Beverly Hills, CA: Sage.

Pettigrew, T. F. (1988). Integration and pluralism. In P. Katz & D. A. Taylor (Eds.), *Eliminating racism: Profiles in controversy* (pp. 19-30). New York: Plenum.

Pettigrew, T. F., Fredrickson, G. M., Knobel, D. T., & Glazer, N. & Veda, R. (Eds.). (1982). *Prejudice: Dimensions of ethnicity.* Cambridge, MA: Harvard University Press.

Phillips, D., & Rathwell, T. (Eds.). (1986). *Health, race and ethnicity.* London: Croom Helm.

Phinney, J. S. (1989). Stages of ethnic identity in minority group adolescence. *Journal of Early Adolescence, 9,* 34-49.

Phinney, J. S. (1990). Ethnic identity in adolescents and adults: Review of research. *Psychological Bulletin, 108,* 499-514.

Phinney, J. S., & Alipuria, L. (1990). Ethnic identity in older adolescents from four ethnic groups. *Journal of Adolescence, 13,* 171-183.

Phinney, J. S., Lochner, B. T., & Murphy, R. (1990). Ethnic identity development and psychological adjustment in adolescence. In A. R. Stiffman & L. E. Davis (Eds.), *Ethnic issues in adolescent mental health* (pp. 53-72). Newbury Park, CA: Sage.

Phinney, J. S., & Rotheram, M. J. (1987a). *Children's ethnic socialization: Pluralism and development.* Newbury Park, CA: Sage.

Phinney, J. S., & Rotheram, M. J. (1987b). Children's ethnic socialization: Themes and implications. In J. S. Phinney & M. J. Rotheram (Eds.), *Children's ethnic socialization: Pluralism and development* (pp. 274-292). Newbury Park, CA: Sage.

Phinney, J. S., & Tarver, S. (1988). Ethnic identity search and commitment in black and white eighth graders. *Journal of Early Adolescence, 8,* 265-277.

Pinkow, L. C., Ehrlich, H. J., & Purvis, R. D. (1990). *Group tensions on American colleges: 1989.* Institute Working Paper No. 1. Baltimore, MD: National Institute Against Prejudice and Violence.

Pleck, J. H. (1976). The male sex role: Definitions, problems and sources of change. *Journal of Social Issues, 32* (3), 155-164.

Ponterotto, J. G. (1988). Racial consciousness development among white counselor trainees: A stage model. *Journal of Multicultural Counseling and Development, 16,* 146-156.

Ponterotto, J. G. (1991). The nature of prejudice revisited: Implications for counseling intervention. *Journal of Counseling and Development, 70,* 216-224.

Ponterotto, J. G., & Benesch, K. F. (1988). An organizational framework for understanding the role of culture in counseling. *Journal of Counseling and Development, 66,* 237-142.

Ponterotto, J. G., Burkard, A., D'Onofrio, A. A., Dubuisson, A., Heenehan, M., Millstein, B., Parisi, M., Rath, J., & Sax, G. (1993). *Development and validation of the Quick Discrimination Index (QDI).* Manuscript submitted for publication.

Ponterotto, J. G., & Casas, J. M. (1987). In search of multicultural competence within counselor education programs. *Journal of Counseling and Development, 65,* 430-434.

Ponterotto, J. G., & Casas, J. M. (1991). *Handbook of racial/ethnic minority counseling research.* Springfield, IL: Charles C Thomas.

Ponterotto, J. G., & Furlong, M. J. (1985). Evaluating counselor effectiveness: A critical review of rating scale instruments. *Journal of Counseling Psychology, 32,* 597-616.

Ponterotto, J. G., Lewis, D. E., & Bullington, R. (1990). *Affirmative action on campus.* San Francisco, CA: Jossey-Bass.

Ponterotto, J. G., Rieger, B. P., Barrett, A., & Sparks, R. (in press). Assessing multicultural counseling competence: A review of instrumentation. *Journal of Counseling and Development.*

Ponterotto, J. G., & Sabnani, H. B. (1989). "Classics" in multicultural counseling: A systematic five-year content analysis. *Journal of Multicultural Counseling and Development, 17,* 23-37.

Ponterotto, J. G., Sanchez, C. M., & Magids, D. M. (1991, August). *Initial development and validation of the Multicultural Counseling Awareness Scale (MCAS).* Paper presented at the annual meeting of the American Psychological Association, San Francisco.

Ponterotto, J. G. & Wise, S. L. (1987). Construct validity of the Racial Identity Attitude Scale. *Journal of Counseling Psychology, 34,* 218-223.

Pope-Davis, D. B., & Ottavi, T. M. (1992). The influence of white racial identity attitudes on racism among faculty members: A preliminary examination. *Journal of College Student Development, 33,* 389-394.

Pope-Davis, D. B., & Ottavi, T. M. (in press). The relationship between racism and racial identity among white Americans: A replication and extension. *Journal of Counseling and Development.*

Pyant, C. T., & Yanico, B. J. (1991). Relationship of racial identity and gender-role attitudes to black women's psychological well-being. *Journal of Counseling Psychology, 38,* 315-322.

Ramirez, M. III (1991). *Psychotherapy and counseling with minorities: A cognitive approach to individual and cultural differences.* New York: Pergamon.

Rebecca, M., Hefner, R., & Oleshansky, B. (1976). A model of sex role transcendence. *Journal of Social Issues, 32* (3), 197-206.

Report of the National Advisory Commission on Civil Disorders. (1968). New York: Bantam Books.

Ridley, C. R. (1989). Racism in counseling as an adverse behavioral process. In P. B. Pedersen, J. G. Draguns, W. J. Lonner, & J. E. Trimble (Eds.), *Counseling across cultures* (3rd ed.) (pp. 55-77). Honolulu: University of Hawaii Press.

Robbins, R. H. (1973). Identity, culture and behavior. In J. J. Honigmann (Ed.), *Handbook of social and cultural anthropology* (pp. 97-124). Chicago: Rand McNally.

Roberts, M. C., & Peterson, L. (Eds.). (1984). *Prevention of problems in childhood: Psychological research and applications.* New York: John Wiley.

Rose, P. I. (1964). *They and we: Racial and ethnic relations in the United States.* New York: Random House.

Rosen, H., & Rosen, D. (1962). *But not next door.* New York: Ivan Obolensky.

Ruiz, A. S. (1990). Ethnic identity: Crisis and resolution. *Journal of Multicultural Counseling and Development, 18,* 29-40.

Sabnani, H. B., & Ponterotto, J. G. (1992). Racial/ethnic minority instrumentation in counseling research: A review, critique, and recommendations. *Measurement and Evaluation in Counseling and Development, 24,* 161-187.

Sabnani, H. B., Ponterotto, J. G., & Borodovsky, L. G. (1991). White racial identity development and cross-cultural counselor training: A stage model. *The Counseling Psychologist, 19,* 76-102.

Schenkel, S., & Marcia, J. E. (1972). Attitudes toward premarital intercourse in determining ego identity status in college women. *Journal of Personality, 40,* 472-482.

Schniedwind, N., & Davidson, E. (1983). *Open minds to equality.* Englewood Cliffs, NJ: Prentice Hall.

Sears, D. (1988). Symbolic racism. In P. A. Katz & D. A. Taylor (Eds.), *Eliminating racism: Profiles in controversy* (pp. 53-84). New York: Plenum.

Sedlacek, W. E., & Brooks, G. C., Jr. (1970). Measuring racial attitudes in a situational context. *Psychological Reports, 27,* 971-980.

Sedlacek, W. E., & Brooks, G. C., Jr. (1976). *Racism in American education: A model for change.* Chicago: Nelson-Hall.

Segal, M. H., Dasen, P. R., Berry, J. W., & Poortinga, Y. H. (Eds.). (1990). *Human behavior in global perspective: An introduction to cross-cultural psychology.* Elmsford, NY: Pergamon.

Sherif, M., & Sherif, C. (1953). *Groups in harmony and tension.* New York: Harper.

Sherman, R. L. (1990). Intergroup conflict on high school campuses. *Journal of Multicultural Counseling and Development, 18,* 11-18.

Shiman, D. A. (1979). *The prejudice book: Activities for the classroom.* New York: Anti-Defamation League of B'nai B'rith.

Simpson, G. E., & Yinger, J. M. (1985). *Racial and cultural minorities: An analysis of prejudice and discrimination* (5th ed.). New York: Plenum.

Skillings, J. H., & Dobbins, J. E. (1991). Racism as a disease: Etiology and treatment implications. *Journal of Counseling and Development, 70,* 206-212.

Smith, E. J. (1989). Black racial identity development: Issues and concerns. *The Counseling Psychologist, 17,* 277-288.

Smith, E. J. (1991). Ethnic identity development: Toward the development of a theory within the context of majority/minority status. *Journal of Counseling and Development, 70,* 181-188.

Smith, L. (1963). *Killers of the dream.* Garden City, NY: Anchor Books.

Sobol, T. (1990, April). *A curriculum of inclusion: Strengthening students' understanding of one another, our culture and the world.* Paper presented to the New York State Board of Regents, Albany, New York.

Sodowsky, G. R., Taffe, R. C., Gutkin, T., & Wise, S. L. (1992). *Development and applications of the Multicultural Counseling Inventory.* Manuscript submitted for publication.

Stagner, R. (1987). Foreword. In J. Boucher, D. Landis, & K. A. Clark (Eds.), *Ethnic conflict: International perspectives* (pp. 7-16). Newbury Park, CA: Sage.

Stalvey, L. M. (1970). *The education of a WASP.* New York: William Morrow.

Sue, D. W. (1992). The challenge of multiculturalism: The road less traveled. *American Counselor, 1* (1), 6-14.

Sue, D. W., & Sue, D. (1990). *Counseling the culturally different: Theory and practice* (2nd ed.). New York: John Wiley.

Tajfel, H. (1970). Experiments in intergroup discrimination. *Scientific American, 223* (2), 96-102.

Tajfel, H. (1974). Social identity and intergroup behavior. *Social Science Information, 13* (2).

Tajfel, H. (1978). *The social psychology of minorities.* New York: Minority Rights Group.

Taub, D. J., & McEwen, M. K. (1992). The relationship of racial identity attitudes to autonomy and mature interpersonal relationships in black and white undergraduate women. *Journal of College Student Development, 33,* 439-446.

Terry, R. W. (1981). The negative impact on white values. In B. P. Bowser & R. G. Hunt (Eds.), *Impacts of racism on white Americans* (pp. 119-151). Beverly Hills, CA: Sage.

Thomas, C. W. (1971). *Boys no more.* Beverly Hills, CA: Glencoe.

Thompson, E. T., & Hughes, E. C. (1958). *Race: Individual collective behavior.* Glencoe, IL: Free Press.

Tokar, D. M., & Swanson, J. L. (1991). An investigation of the validity of Helms' (1984) model of white racial identity development. *Journal of Counseling Psychology, 38,* 296-301.

Triandis, H. C., Vassiliou, V., Vassiliou, G., Tanaka, Y., & Shanmugam, A. V. (1972). *The analysis of subjective culture.* New York: John Wiley.

Troyna, B., & Hatcher, R. (1992). *Racism in children's lives: A study of mainly-white Primary schools.* London: Routledge.

van Dijk, T. A. (1987). *Communicating racism: Ethnic prejudice in thought and talk.* Newbury Park, CA: Sage.

Waterman, A. (1984). *The psychology of individualism.* New York: Praeger.

Walsh, D. (1988). Critical thinking to reduce prejudice. *Social Education, 52,* 280-282.

"When tensions rise." (1992, September 2). *USA Today,* p. 9A.

White, J. L., & Parham, T. A. (1990). *The psychology of blacks: An African-American perspective* (2nd ed.). Englewood, NJ: Prentice Hall.

White, T. J., & Sedlacek, W. E. (1987). White student attitudes toward blacks and Hispanics: Programming implications. *Journal of Multicultural Counseling and Development, 15,* 171-183.

Wirth, L. (1945). The problem of minority groups. In R. Linton (Ed.), *The science of man in world crisis* (pp. 347-372). New York: Columbia University Press.

Wrenn, C. G. (1962). The culturally encapsulated counselor. *Harvard Educational Review, 32,* 444-449.

Wrenn, C. G. (1985). Afterward: The culturally encapsulated counselor revisited. In P. B. Pedersen (Ed.), *Handbook of cross-cultural counseling and therapy* (pp. 323-329). Westport, CT: Greenwood Press.

Wright, D. J. (1990). Affirmative action: The second step. In J. G. Ponterotto, D. E. Lewis, & R. Bullington (Eds.), *Affirmative action on campus* (pp. 89-96). San Francisco, CA: Jossey-Bass.

Yinger, J. M. (1976). Ethnicity in complex societies. In L. A. Coser & O. N. Larsen (Eds.), *The uses of controversy in sociology* (pp. 197-216). New York: Free Press.

Name Index

Subject Index

Asian-American identity development. *See* Minority identity development

Black racial identity development. *See* Minority identity development

Counselor roles in fighting racism, 87-97
Culture, definition of, 7

Ethnicity, definition of, 6-7

Fight of Flight Response Theory of Racial Stress, 80-82

Hispanic American ethnic identity development. *See* Minority identity development

Identity development:
Erickson's model, 40

Marcia's model, 40-41
Instruments, guidelines for selecting, 143-144
Instruments to assess multicultural counseling competence:
Cross-Cultural Counseling Inventory-Revised (CCI-R), 142
Multicultural Counseling Awareness Scale (MCAS), 142
Multicultural Counseling Inventory (MCI), 142
Multicultural Awareness/Knowledge/Skills Survey (MAKSS), 142-143
Instruments to assess racial identity:
African Self-Consciousness Scale (ASCS), 140
Developmental Inventory of Black Consciousness (DIB-C), 140
Racial Identity Attitude Scale (RIAS), 140
White Racial Identity Attitude Scale (WRIAS), 141
Instruments to assess racism and prejudice:
Institutional Racism Scale (IRS), 138-139
Modern Racism Scale (MRS), 138

About the Authors

Joseph G. Ponterotto is Associate Professor and Coordinator of the Counseling Psychology Program at Fordham University's Graduate School of Education (Lincoln Center Campus). Prior to his arrival at Fordham in 1987, he was Assistant Professor at the University of Nebraska-Lincoln. He holds an M.A. in Counseling and a Ph.D. in Counseling Psychology from the University of California at Santa Barbara.

Dr. Ponterotto has served on multicultural-focused national committees of the American Psychological Association and the American Counseling Association. He is the senior author of the *Handbook of Racial/Ethnic Minority Counseling Research* and the senior editor of *Affirmative Action on Campus* . He is the author of numerous journal articles in the multicultural area and has served on the editorial boards of the *Journal of Counseling Psychology, The Counseling Psychologist, Journal of Multicultural Counseling and Development, Counseling and Values*, and *Educational Psychology Review.*

Paul B. Pedersen is Professor at the School of Education at Syracuse University. He holds an M.S. in Counseling and Student Personnel Psychology from the University of Minnesota and a Ph.D. in Asian Studies, emphasizing Asian psychologies, from Claremont Graduate School. His primary interests include the effects of group differences on interpersonal interaction between cultural and nationality groups in the educational setting, multicultural counseling theory and practice, mediating multicultural conflict, international educational exchange, and intercultural training.

Dr. Pedersen has also taught at the University of Malaya (Indonesia), the University of Minnesota, the University of Hawaii, and Harvard University. He has been a Senior Fellow at the East-West Center, Director of an NIMH Mental Health Training Project, "Developing Interculturally Skilled Counselors," and an international student advisor at the University of Minnesota. He is the author or editor of 21 books, 42 chapters in books, 69 articles and 19 other monograph-length documents.